When the Going Gets Tough

When the Going Gets Tough

A Spirituality For Hard Times

John Wickham, S.J.

NOVALIS

When the Going Gets Tough:
  A Spirituality For Hard Times is published by Novalis.

Cover and layout: Gilles Lepine

© 1994, Novalis, St. Paul University, Ottawa, Canada

Business Office: Novalis, 49 Front St. East, 2nd Floor,
   Toronto, Ontario, M5E 1B3

Editorial Office: Novalis, 223 Main Street, Ottawa, Ontario, K1S 1C4

Legal deposit: 3rd trimester, 1994
   National Library of Canada
   Bibliothèque nationale du Québec

Printed in Canada.

Canadian Cataloguing in Publication Data

Wickham, John F. (John Francis), 1926-
    When the going gets tough: a spirituality for hard times

(Inner journey series)
Includes bibliographical references.
ISBN 2-89088-675-1

    1. Poverty—Religious aspects—Christianity.
2. Poor—Religious aspects—Christianity.
I. Title. II. Series.

BV4647.P6W43 1994   261.8'325   C94-900590-8

NOVALIS

Foreword

The great theologian Karl Rahner once remarked that "poverty" is actually experienced by most people in Western culture today in new forms of insecurity. He went on to insist that this stressful insecurity of ours is much more severe a trial than the shortage of possessions and of consumer goods so usual in former ages (and continuing now in other parts of the world).

Our spiritual tradition on Christian poverty has been focused almost exclusively on choosing to live with insufficiency or near destitution. While our cities and countryside today certainly do include pockets, corners and whole social layers of that kind, these "exceptions" tend to be pushed to the margins. And since most of us aren't suffering in that way, we can easily miss the connection.

For the main text of our modern story speaks, not of "lack," but of "glut." We have too many events to attend, too many consumer goods stacked up on store shelves, too many sorts of fruit and vegetables in our food marts, and too many cars for our parking spaces. Our industries are producing enormous supplies of toxic wastes (it's the negative side of "too much"), and these are polluting our air, land and water—everywhere. We certainly throw away far too much garbage—where "on earth" are we going to put it all?

Moreover, we suffer from too many demands on our time, too much haste and bustle in our lives. We easily grow tired of making so many decisions. And underlying all those choices lurks the insecurity mentioned by Karl Rahner. For endless change is the condition of our affluent lifestyle. Nothing will stay as it is for very long, we fear.

Even when the end of the Cold War has lessened the threat of nuclear bombs, an amazing number of ethnic or political wars and bloody-minded troubles have broken out. Besides, we find ourselves living up to our necks in debt. We sense that the ground under our feet may easily fall away. Our retirement plans are perhaps a deception. Those we elect can't be trusted to protect us (too many of them are mainly influenced by powerful lobbies).

Unemployment has become a scourge in more and more families. And so we find our world undergoing "hard times" again. The good news is that our economy is beginning to crawl back from the edge of depression. But the bad news, as we are so often reminded on our newscasts, is that the lost jobs will not be returning. If so, what is that going to mean for ordinary people?

It seems clear to me that we need to renew our spiritual attitude towards possessions, indebtedness, our ways of participating collectively, our relationship with people in other parts of the world, as well as towards the "main text" and the "margins" at home. Most of all, we must learn how to cope better with the underlying insecurities that threaten our peace and our freedom for creative action. This short essay is meant to address our new economic facts from the standpoint of Christian faith.

I cannot, of course, pretend to supply ready-made answers to the questions that arise, least of all the economic ones. But I do want to formulate those questions in ways that may speak directly to what concerns our spiritual resources. I hope to focus more accurately on what matters for us. And I desire to bring the wealth of Scripture and our faith tradition to bear on our real situation. That, quite simply, is the meaning of my title, A Spirituality for Hard Times.

After an overview of our current realities as they have been talked about recently (especially by non-experts), I will look at the teachings of Christ on ownership, and then briefly at the various ways in which the Lord's teaching has been put into practice down the centuries.

That should enable us to see more clearly what is special and even unique about the economic situation that concerns us today. Then we may consider new approaches in spirituality for dealing effectively with this world, a world that holds us in its powerful and often frightening embrace.

J.W.
Montreal, 1994.

Contents

1

Why Do We Have Hard Times?

The Great Depression of the 1930's is part of my childhood memory—it belongs to the time that shaped me unforgettably. Our family never suffered severely, but the economic downturn was all around us. I was three years old in 1929, too young to hear "the crash" on the stock-market, but old enough to grow into "hard times" as if they were the nature of things: no coins in my pocket, an atmosphere of thrift and scrimping, of putting pennies in a piggy bank—even the thrill of buying one-cent candies at the local store. I belonged to a family of eight children, the sixth born. We lived in Montreal.

My father was the sort of medical man who spent a lot of his time paying visits to sick people in their homes. He kept a tall telephone by his bed, and if a call came, for example, in January at four a.m. from a family in Verdun whose father had suffered a heart attack, he went out into the frozen night with his little black bag, cranked up his old Buick till it coughed into action, found his way to the address and climbed the icy outdoor stairs to bring them healing (if possible) and some reassurance. He was gifted with a wonderful "bedside manner." But it was authentic: he actually loved his patients, and they gave him much consolation in return.

Today the same family, we all know, would have to call for an ambulance, send their relative to the hospital at once and perhaps wait a long while (after answering lots of questions) before getting news about his condition. Certainly, the actual medical care—the technology of medical science—is much better today. But the insecurity is much worse.

Besides, at present we are covered by medicare in ways no one could have imagined in the 1930's. But our physical and financial advantages, which are considerable, don't really make up for the spiritual malaise that usually accompanies them today.

My father told me once that for many years more than fifty percent of his patients couldn't pay his bills—and in some cases he didn't even send any bills. He had eight hungry mouths to feed at home, but we never starved. The real effect was that he had no chance to become well-off. And he made that choice knowingly. For he experienced his medical practice as a vocation.

The poor had a claim on him, he felt. It was a pleasure for him to serve them. He didn't really feel insecure. Rather, he felt blessed. His life was filled with the enduring value of what he could do for others. St. Mary's Hospital, where he was a founding doctor, and also the Montreal Convalescent Home (now a "Hospital") were so worthwhile!

The memory of those times enables me to reflect upon our current situation from a different perspective. It helps me to see the novelty of what is going on right now.

Our insecurities, I think, are connected with our spiritual attitudes. But our spiritual responses are perhaps not yet focused very well upon the new facts we face. We are reacting on the basis of an earlier, rather different economic reality—like the one my father had to endure. Those earlier ways of dealing with impoverishment were admirable, but they don't easily square with our new situation. It was an excellent response in its time, but limited to special circumstances that are no longer valid.

In short, my conviction is that our spiritual tradition is much richer than we imagine when we restrict our ideas to former situations alone. It's like trying to cope with modern data by counting on our fingers (when computers are available—and essential in view of the facts we have to face). Or better, it's like a cavalry charge against a fleet of high-powered tanks.

Even more to the point, it's like hammering together a log cabin on a site destined for a skyscraper: we need a new model in our minds, a more sensible blueprint. We must clarify our vision. And then, more deeply and more confidently, we need to explore the resources available to us in our spiritual tradition. But first and foremost we must try to locate ourselves in the economic situation which we actually face.

Three Interpretations Often Heard

Whenever the subject of "hard times" is introduced, there will be no lack of opinions, of course. In popular conversation—and even from the mouths of specialists—a large range of views may be expected. And sometimes these opinions are given very strongly—as if to end all discussion.

What follows, then, will be a short list of what I've heard repeated many times. Not that these views are all false. There is likely some truth in all of them—along with the evident falsehoods. My purpose in putting them down here, gathered under three headings, is simply to assist readers in thinking the matter through. Not that this little list will exhaust the topic. I merely want to run through the more frequently mentioned opinions.

1. Moralistic Views

According to this approach, hard times are simply caused by human greed. Our recession results from too many people seeking wealth selfishly—without any care for the common good of all. There are several variants of this opinion (which treats a whole people on the model of a single person):

a) God punishes all of us for the sins of greed in our midst. After a while, our whole economy tends to give way and hard times are the result.

b)   Our economic system itself is based on the self-interested efforts of many individuals working in competition. Often this tends to produce good effects, but it may also veer into recession.

c)   Too many members of society want to live on handouts, and our economy can't support so much non-productive laziness.

d)   Corrupt practices by big corporations, supported by politicians "in their pocket," lead to the mess we are in. The rich get richer and the poor get poorer.

More variants of this kind could perhaps be added. But the theology, not just the economic theory, implied by these views (they are the ones most often brought to my attention) are rather wobbly, to say the least. The God who punishes? And if so, why make the poor suffer more than the rich?

We would also want to know where the evidence (statistics?) may be found for claims about the moral attitudes of those living at the bottom of our income ladder. Edmund Burke, I seem to remember, once said that you can't bring a whole people into court ("indict a nation") and the same would apply to classes or groups of persons whether at the foot, middle or top of society.

2. Fatalistic Views

The conviction in this case is that the relentless cycle of a rising and falling economy is inevitable. No efforts to prevent or control it will work: "What goes up must come down." Enjoy the fat years, then, but get ready for the lean years—since they can't be avoided. There are many variants of this view as well:

a)   Our modern industrial form of production tends to force-feed the economic system. Great advances might occur, but severe downturns will follow of necessity. It's "dialectical": going too far in one direction results in the opposite tendency after a certain time.

b)   The fixed laws of modern science at work in our economy, one of which is a cyclical return of recessions. We must accept this scientific view of economic development, like it or not, even though it makes recessions inevitable.

c) So far, all the theories of economics put forward have proven to be, at least partly, false. Perhaps what is involved are mysterious mood changes that grip the general public. No one seems to know why the public mood changes.

Some of the above is anti-intellectual, but under many of the words used lurks a good dose of fatalism. And that is a kind of spirituality—a bad kind, one that must be resisted.

The assumptions behind fatalism are various. Some hold that our physical world always takes "revenge" on us: industry goes against "the nature of things," and that provokes negative reactions—like recessions. Other assumptions have to do with the "laws of modern science," but whatever may be said about certainty in the physical sciences does not appear to apply to economics.

Other assumptions, on the other side, refer to blind forces operating in human society as a whole. This is very discouraging. It sounds wise, perhaps, but it eliminates any belief in divine caring, any sense of worthwhile tasks given to human beings on earth, and any hope of making better arrangements in our economy.

Finally, human ignorance itself (which is true enough) can be used to beat us into submission. But just because there will always be much that we don't know, it doesn't follow that we can't learn more than before. In our human history there has been an undeniable growth in understanding and a build-up of real and effective knowledge. Experts in all these matters may be poor masters for us, but they are certainly excellent servants.

3. Social Views

Under this heading we find the opinions of those who blame individual ownership for most of our woes. They think very extensive governmental interference is essential. Here are a few variants often heard in our time:

a) Adam Smith's "invisible hand" theory, which was widely believed, leads to hard times. Smith imagined that, by God's hidden plan, universal benefits would come from the work of many selfishly competing individuals. But the actual result has been a series of painful recessions. Instead, an active government must see to it that false tendencies are corrected, an overall distribution system put in place, and a safety net provided for the disadvantaged.

b) In the nineteenth century a "laissez-faire" (hands off) attitude prevailed almost everywhere in the West. This led the government in England to do little or nothing for starving people during the potato famine in Ireland (food was actually being shipped out of Ireland at the time). That was well-intentioned madness, we think today.

c) Finally, President Roosevelt introduced his New Deal economics during the Great Depression of the 1930's. The government should take many initiatives: it should control the money supply, change tax structures, intervene in labour-management disputes, introduce mega-projects, combine public and private enterprises, alter interest rates, and so forth. The Great Depression seemed to prove the need for this sort of action—once and for all.

Those three positions cover a lot of territory. What are we to make of it all? Certainly the New Deal approach, while carrying with it some general truths few would want to deny, was not as successful as some maintain and has not proven its value in recent decades. Government parties try to claim the credit when the economy does well, and to sidestep any blame when it performs rather poorly, in recent years.

It seems clear enough that we need both dedicated (and highly motivated) businessmen as well as careful watchdogs in government. And even if we could get a first-class combination of these two elements, plus wise policies for the money supply, new approaches to worker participation, new experiments in management and styles of leadership, and so on—we would still encounter other difficulties. And we are very far from being able to put all these factors together.

"Competition in international markets" is an oft-repeated phrase today—held over our heads like a threat, and further undermining our security. And "world-class technologies" always seem to call for fewer jobs and special training for which almost no one is prepared.

Recovery will come, we are being told, but unemployment will continue to rise as well. None of our economic theories in the past had to face that bleak prospect. Will new, mind-boggling theories soon appear?—views that try to take our present difficulties into account? In any case, that is not my task (nor would I be capable of handling it).

Some Spiritual Responses

What I do plan to consider here are the spiritual attitudes we might adopt in view of the facts confronting us today, especially when those facts include a good portion of ignorance and frustration on many sides. At this stage I close my review of the various opinions I have rehearsed by mentioning some of the responses I heard when they were discussed.

One point made by a number of persons was that we don't need to be miserable during a recession. Sadness or anger, bitterness and resentment, accusing and blaming result from too much materialism. The spiritual approach we could call "materialistic" refers to our Western tendency to demand wealth for ourselves as a sort of right. We can easily define ourselves as people meant to be well-off. But our spiritual tradition teaches us the very opposite, of course.

The ticket to happiness, then, is detachment from owning expensive goods. Attachment to wealth (even in desire alone) is a ticket to misery. During hard times we are given an opportunity to find true happiness—for some, this may be a new discovery, a breakthrough. Perhaps God has to stop us in our tracks in order to teach us the way to freedom.

My own caution in regard to this truth is that it can, all too easily, be turned into a method of consoling "spiritually" those who are being marginalized in a material sense. In practice, religious faith may be used as a way of avoiding difficult public issues, of refusing to take a stand or look for better financial policies to support.

In discussions I attended, some members present insisted, then, that we ought not to "romanticize poverty" (meaning destitution, or near destitution). In fact, there is often a social stigma associated with low-level income. If you're not successful, there must be something wrong with you—or so it may be felt without being spoken.

Another excellent point, I thought, was directed against the narrowness of some moral thinking in our midst. For example, since individualism is notoriously overdone in Western society, there is a great need today to give priority to the common good and to discover grounds for common action. In short, the wider context of our economic life ought to become the framework of our discussions.

Beyond that, there is the question of openness to new developments—of studying the facts more carefully, of pondering the issues, and of following up points of special concern. In other words, our strong moral commitments should not cut us off from searching for the truth. One member quoted Bernard Lonergan's saying that "ignorance causes more hardship than greed."

Others stressed the fact that the meaning of "rich" and "poor" varies so much around the world. Many of us realize that for people in less developed countries even those among us whom we call "poor" are actually "rich." In a sense, many in other parts of the world are trying to get where we are—and when they do, they will have to face the problems now afflicting us. Perhaps they are happier on the average, and more concerned for others, than we are.

But we can't make notions like these an excuse for ignoring the systemic needs of those in less developed lands. Our recently acquired global awareness adds the key point that all parts of the earth are interdependent. What this means is that the West "lives off" the East, and the North off the South.

What we've run through so rapidly in this chapter seems to me a necessary start for our discussion. But it can be no more than a beginning. Now we need to turn more carefully to our religious tradition on the subject of poverty. What has the Church learned from its many centuries of trying to live the Gospel faithfully? And what can be the meaning of what Jesus says so emphatically about the poor?

2

What Does Christ Teach About Poverty?

It may help all of us to take a fresh dip in the bracing waters of Jesus' own words. Make it a "skinny dip" all by yourself—so as to get the feel of his sayings without any protective covering. What I mean is that you pick up your copy of the New Testament and read over—as receptively as you can—the words that you've heard so often before, but take them now as if spoken to you for the first time.

It's clear enough that Jesus' teaching on poverty is central, not an extra, in his Gospel message of salvation. In other words, if we are to be Christian at all, we will have to come to terms with what the Lord presents to us on this head. So we don't want to "explain it away." (I should make it clear that I'm referring to lay Christians living in the world, and not just to vowed members of religious orders and congregations.)

Jesus doesn't mince matters. Consider the following, for example: "Whoever of you does not renounce all [s]he has cannot be my disciple" (Lk 14:33). Please try that out on your heart. Surely it comes to us with a sense of shock.

What could it possibly mean? Of course, as with other Scriptural topics, we should ponder each passage in relation to all the others. Jesus, we recall, does not speak at a theoretical level or teach like a university professor. He responds to concrete situations. He challenges each one. He calls us forth. He did not write a treatise on poverty—in fact, we have nothing in writing from the Lord, only faithfully remembered words spoken on many different occasions.

If we review the Gospels as a whole, we discover that very little on poverty can be found in John. But in Matthew, Mark and Luke it appears as a central theme. Accordingly, I will take up the main texts in these three "synoptic" Gospels alone. (Beginning with Matthew, I shall not always repeat the parallel passages in Mark or Luke, but I'll list these whenever they seem significant so that you may ponder the differences in tone and context, if you wish.)

Poverty In St. Matthew

It is Matthew, of course, who presents the Sermon on the Mount as a summary of the basics of Jesus' teaching, starting with the Eight Beatitudes. And "poverty of spirit" is given the place of honour at the front.

Unlike the Pharisees, Jesus doesn't stress the Law (although we must not imply that he despises the Law—on the contrary). Instead, he chooses to praise those who have received the various graces of the Kingdom of Heaven—God's reigning amid this world. And like the other Beatitudes, poverty is a grace which makes us happy: "How happy are the poor in spirit: theirs is the kingdom of heaven!" (Mt 5:3; Lk 6:20,24).

How blest are those who know they need God! The Kingdom belongs to them. They own it! They have given up any ambition to possess a worldly kingdom, to dominate others, to acquire the material means for putting others under their power, or for exercising any kind of superiority on earth.

This makes them free from any enslavement. It also opens them to the (very different) kind of belonging that comes with the active reigning of the Father in the hearts of hum; in this world—as this may be seen in Jesus himself.

My expansion of Matthew's phrase should not d if you prefer another way of responding to it. I simply want to indicate how I see Matthew "placing" the words of Jesus on poverty as the keystone of his message about God's Kingdom— the divine way of being present among human beings in this world. (The parallel in Luke is quite different—whole books have been written on this difference, so I'll leave it at that.)

But since Matthew used the term "in spirit" and I'm writing here about spirituality, let me say briefly that a great deal of nonsense has been repeated to the effect that the real message is given in Luke (who says, "Happy are the poor") and only a watered-down version in Matthew (who uses, "Happy are the poor in spirit"). To me, that opinion seems to miss the point entirely.

By "spirit" Matthew certainly means what the Holy Spirit has brought about most effectively in the very heart of believers—so as to change their whole way of living in this world. I wish to use the word "spirituality" in its original sense of a whole way of life transformed and energized by the Holy Spirit.

If someone takes the terms "spirit," "spiritual" and therefore "spirituality" to mean a cop-out from reality, or a turning inward from the hard facts of life on earth, or abandoning the crunch of concrete decisions about destitution, injustice and marginalization, or whatever, then a basic misreading of Matthew has corrupted his text, I think. I agree that the worst denial of spirituality can be made its very definition, but to reject the term would mean the loss of an excellent word. (Shall we omit the word "love" because so many people abuse it?)

I prefer to use the phrase "poverty of spirit" to mean something even more difficult and more demanding than a merely external separation from material goods, namely our total dedication interiorly to the service of God and others (through the grace of the Spirit who transforms us) in such a way as to effectively change our behaviour in the real world of goods and relationships to which we are called.

To put this more simply, "spiritual" refers in Scripture and in our faith tradition to a whole way of life under the leading of the Spirit. "Poverty of spirit," then, would mean a radical transformation of the same kind in relation to possessions. It can make sense of the saying I quoted above, "Whoever of you does not renounce all he has cannot be my disciple." Our faith itself must begin with a radical reorientation towards wealth.

Since St. Matthew has grasped this essential point in the teaching of Jesus, it seems peculiar (to put it mildly) to argue that he is trying to water down the Gospel. Perhaps those who argue that way are actually referring, not to the evangelist, but to people who misinterpret him in ways that are convenient to their continuing desire for riches.

On what he has given us from the start, then, St. Matthew builds up a remarkable edifice of teachings on poverty. As a simple example of what follows in ordinary life, Jesus urges us to give and lend freely what we possess (Mt 5:42). He also suggests that we store up riches in heaven rather than on earth (Mt 6:19-21; Lk 12:32-34). A beautiful piece follows on our tendency to worry about material things: Don't be anxious, he says; imitate the birds and the flowers in the service they give to God; in any case, your Father in heaven knows perfectly well what you need (Mt 6:25-34; Lk 12:22-31). So, peacefully do your best to earn your living, but (in the midst of doing that) it's essential to develop a habit of trusting God beyond anything else.

All this is found in the Sermon on the Mount itself. A little further on (Mt 8:20; Lk 9:57-62), the same evangelist lets fall another stunner: "The Son of Man has nowhere to lay his head," Jesus tells us. Apparently for a time he did have a house at his disposal in Capernaum, the scholars point out. In any case, he was ready to give that up, too. After leaving home in Nazareth, he felt free to plunge into his public teaching in Galilee and then in Judea without caring about the duties of a householder. He didn't claim a home of his own but lived wherever anyone would put him up.

A small circle of his disciples, whom he called to follow him about as he moved around Palestine, were exceptional. It seems clear that the majority of his "disciples" (meaning both men and women) continued to live at home and that Jesus expected them to do so. They were obviously the ones from whom he and his twelve apostles begged alms. Nowhere does he say that his teaching required all his disciples to give up their homes in the world and live from day to day on alms—such an idea would be ridiculous. Nor does he say or imply that the vast majority who continued to lead normal lives at home were "second rank" disciples.

Martha, with her brother Lazarus and her sister Mary, was a well-to-do householder, it appears, at whose home Jesus sometimes stayed. Nowhere does he tell them to sell everything off in order to "hit the streets." They belonged to the large number of those who followed his teaching.

That Jesus expects most people (special vocations are an exception which proves the rule) to retain their possessions and to act responsibly in making careful arrangements for the material upkeep of themselves and their families—this must have seemed too plain to mention in so many words. Must the obvious be harped upon? As St. Ignatius remarked in another connection (that after his resurrection Jesus appeared first to his mother), God assumes we "have understanding."

No, what Jesus wanted to emphasize—even to the point of shocking his hearers out of their smugness—was the total freedom from greed, from an anxiety over material goods that so often gets control of human beings living in this world. Is it any different today? And yet this radical detachment is the entry-point to the kingdom of heaven on earth, which Jesus revealed to be near at hand. "Be converted, and change your attitude completely," he said in announcing his good news. The kingdom of God is right here, available to you, if you say Yes to the grace that is now being offered (see Mk 1:15).

The spiritual freedom which Jesus had in mind is illustrated in another saying. Give without expecting to be paid, says Jesus (Mt 10:8b). Then there is his point about even the smallest kindness shown: a glass of water shared with a thirsty stranger will be noticed and rewarded by the Father (Mt 10:42).

Last of all in Matthew's Gospel comes a series of great parables, all of which reveal in different ways the total liberation from enslavement to wealth and possessions that is the hallmark of the kingdom preached by Jesus. The parables of the Hidden Treasure and the Pearl (Mt 13:44-46) bring out the overwhelming desire (Jesus expects all his followers to feel this keen surge of desire) for values that go beyond any kind of materialistic reckoning. For people so graced, worrying over possessions seems utterly absurd.

Jesus enjoys a party. He expects believers to celebrate their happiness together. But many people invited to join them "have more important things to do." "I've bought a new pair of oxen, and they take all my time." (Today we might hear, "I've just bought a brand new car, and I want to try it out on the highway.") In many ways people can define themselves by what they own or what they hope to acquire, and so they don't experience any desire to seek the "treasures in heaven" made possible by the gift of poverty of spirit.

In his parable of the Wedding Feast (Mt 22:1-10; Lk 14:15-24), Jesus notes the frequent refusals of wealthy people to accept the good news. And he directs our attention instead to the many who are marginalized and excluded by those better-off rulers and controllers of worldly power. People "on the outs" are the ones who should be invited. Perhaps they will be ready to receive the gospel message.

In the parable of the Gold Talents, on the other hand, the Lord shocks us again by showing how much is expected of those who have received spiritual gifts (Mt 25:14-30; Lk 19:11-27). Riches "in heaven" can be treated as selfishly as riches "on earth"—and yet that temptation, apparently overcome by those who at first hear the gospel, can all too easily return through the back door in the form of "spiritual power" over others, "spiritual wealth" as making us better than others, "spiritual gifts" as leading us to separate our lives from others and feel no responsibility, no intimate belonging to the humans around us.

This turning in on self on the part of apparently "spiritual" persons is precisely the sin of spiritual pride. In energetic people it sometimes takes the self-righteous form of deciding for others what they ought to do, becoming morally indignant (filled with personal judgments) against the "misbehaviour" of others.

Finally, Matthew shows us in his wonderful parable of the Last Judgment (it shouldn't be taken, I think, as a prediction) how Jesus identifies himself with the very poorest members of society: I lacked decent covering, and you didn't clothe me; I was in prison, and you never visited me! (Mt 25:31-46). The difference between true and false members of the Lord's flock can be discerned by the way they actually treat all those around them in the world. And what kind of criterion does Jesus select? It is clearly his favourite view of poverty that makes the difference.

Poverty In St. Mark

If we turn to the Gospel of St. Mark, four basic teachings stand out (with their parallels in the other two synoptics). When you try to bring the good news to others, Jesus tells us, "take nothing on your journey" (Mk 6:8-9; Mt 10:9-10; Lk 9:3). What is the point of this saying? Don't rely on pressure tactics? Don't try to manipulate others by worldly goods or promises? Be simple and direct, and let the grace of God do the work? Each of us in our prayer will need to feel the exact bearing of these words.

In another place Mark tells the story of Jesus' meeting with the Rich Young Man (Mk 10:17-22; Mt 19:16-30; Lk 18:18-30). This passage has been the occasion of a great deal of misunderstanding. Those who like to extract from Scripture texts a general truth or doctrine that can be applied equally to everyone will perhaps wish to argue that only those who abandon all ownership of goods can become a "real" disciple of Jesus. Is that what the story says?

That abstract generality does not appear. Jesus does challenge a particular man in a special context and situation to make a radical change in his life, true enough (and the man flunked the test). The man's wealth has—despite our first impression of him—become an obstacle to his best desires.

In the passage that follows in Mark (vv.23-31) Jesus does move on to a more general teaching about possessions: "How hard it will be," he exclaims, "for those who have riches to enter the kingdom of God!" We may think of God's kingdom as coming only after death—in the next life. But perhaps Jesus refers to what is already near at hand in the present life. Often the term "rich" refers to persons who invest too much of themselves in what they own.

This deliberate challenge by Jesus packs a lot of punch. In their own "very impoverished" economic conditions, the apostles are thrown for a loss by what the Lord has just said. They "naturally" considered the well-off and the powerful people of their own little world to be especially favoured by God, to be (in fact) much nearer to God than they were themselves. Isn't wealth a divine blessing? Isn't it given to those whom God wishes to honour more than the vast numbers of the have-nots, such as themselves?

Perhaps we ought to reflect carefully whether this is not our own assumption most of the time. If my reader should be an exception (by the grace of God), then do not the majority of our fellow citizens appear to agree with the apostles? Who, after all, buy most of the lottery tickets? Is it not those at the lower end of the income pole—because they assume that the best event that could possibly happen to them would be to become rich?

Jesus does not think so. His teaching is the opposite of that view. But his apostles had a hard time taking it in. Could the Lord be serious? If the rich are not easily able to get into the kingdom of heaven, then who could be saved?

Jesus tells them, the poor have a much better chance. And his view is evidently that we ought to adopt the attitude of those poor people who don't become bitter or resentful at their lot but have become liberated from the worst obstacles to union with God.

This seems to me to be a fair assessment of what this text is saying. How do you respond to it? What do you yourself make of Jesus' teaching on poverty?

On another scale, and "incidentally," Mark gives us the little story of the Widow's Mite (Mk 12:41-44; Lk 21:1-4). Our Lord loved to upset the widespread value systems around him. He also liked to take a fresh approach to the actual treatment of persons by the divine Father. The gifts of the poor and the gifts of the rich, he notes, are weighted on different scales in heaven. He recommends that we adopt the divine scales—our human scales are usually faulty.

Poverty In St. Luke

With the exception of two passages which he shares with Matthew, the texts on poverty in Luke's Gospel have a special tone, it seems to me. At the beginning of this chapter I quoted the key phrase (Lk 14:33) that has always spoken to me most powerfully on the importance of poverty in Jesus' teaching: "'In the same way,' concluded Jesus, 'none of you can be my disciple unless [s]he gives up everything [s]he has'" (Good News Bible).

The phrase itself comes at the end of a longer passage (14:25-33) which the editor of the translation entitles, "The Cost of Being a Disciple." This I take to be typical of St. Luke, who is concerned (it seems to me) about the spiritual formation of new Christians. In verse 26 we read: "Whoever comes to me cannot be my disciple unless he loves me more than he loves his father and his mother, his wife and his children, his brothers and his sisters, and himself as well." In verse 28, "If one of you is planning to build a tower, he sits down first and works out what it will cost . . . ." So, figure it out for yourself. What will it cost you to become a real disciple of Jesus? The answer is, It will cost you everything you possess.

Before this wonderful passage (located at the heart of his Gospel), Luke gives us three preparatory texts. After it four further texts (all of them in chapter 16) put together an extended reflection on the practical meaning of Jesus' teaching for us.

An early chapter (Lk 4:16-21; Mt 11:4-5) introduces us to the theme when Jesus picks up a great prophetic saying in Isaiah (61:1) and applies it to himself," (God) has chosen me to bring good news to the poor!" This reveals the profound meditation of Jesus on the ways of God with Israel. He had been shaped and formed (certainly first of all by his mother) in the deepest knowledge and holiness of the Hebrew Scriptures. No doubt, it was from those spiritual depths that his teaching on poverty emerged.

Next in Luke comes the unique parable of the Rich Fool (12:13-21). This is a negative example, one that reveals the blindness and ignorance of those enslaved by riches. And early in his 14th chapter (vv.12-14) we receive the positive illustration, "When you give a feast, invite the poor."

Then, after the key saying mentioned, his 16th chapter begins and ends with parables—like book-ends. The parable of the Crafty Steward (1-8) tells us how to use the goods and benefits supplied us by God in our lives. The shock in this case seems meant to awaken us to our opportunities for action.

The following collection of sayings (9-13) underlines the importance of getting free from enslavement to wealth in order to act shrewdly in handling our resources. Jesus typically gives us, not only one, but two principles to link together (like his "simple as a dove, cunning as a serpent"). Here they are total freedom from riches, and a subtle wisdom in putting wealth to work for the kingdom of God.

Two other verses (14-15) insist on the difference in God's values. Then, to end his discourse, the great parable of the Rich Man and Lazarus is set before us. This beautiful story, elaborated with ironies as it is, raises the teaching on poverty to a sublime level. Starting with a haunting picture of injustice on earth, it leads on to the glorious divine reversal of human judgments. And the rejection of Jesus' teaching on poverty, and of Jesus himself, by the world in which his historical life was led, is combined with a triumphant sense of the Lord's rightness, fidelity and truth—in the "bosom of Abraham."

Briefly to conclude this rapid review of passages on poverty in the synoptic Gospels, may I repeat how important it is that every reader take time to ponder each passage and to reflect on the ways in which all the texts may be related together to give us a larger—and a deeper—estimate of this central theme.

What next occurs, of course, are daunting questions about how a faithful believer in Jesus may try to express such a mystery in daily life today. But the best approach, it seems to me, will be to look first at the main efforts made by devoted Christians down the centuries to develop ways of life in the world which might exemplify "holy poverty."

3

How
Was Poverty
Practised
In The Past?

A great deal of water has flowed under the bridge of Christian striving to be faithful to evangelical poverty. It's not as though it hasn't been tried! In fact, down the centuries fervent believers have experimented with just about everything we might imagine—even going beyond our wildest dreams.

Think of St. Simeon Stylites, for example, who stood for many years on top of a pillar, or the hermit St. Onofrio, who braved the elements in nothing but his long-grown body hair, or St. Anthony Abbot, who bricked himself up for twelve or more years in an abandoned fort. Poverty was often combined with the most extravagant kinds of suffering. It was understood by St. Ignatius, at his conversion, as a form of penance.

A radical call to poverty, then, was seen as an essential feature of Christian life. Those who received the grace of conversion to Christ often desired to follow his teachings "literally." In different historical periods these economic experiments took many different forms, of course. Only a few of them became widely accepted by others.

In this chapter I want to look more closely at three major variants, the monastic, the mendicant and the active forms of Christian poverty. These three, I believe, have been the most remarkable and the most influential efforts in our history to give a practical and enduring embodiment to Jesus' words. Because of their lived-out quality over many centuries and the large number of persons who devoted themselves to these "ways of life," they deserve careful consideration here.

At once we notice that all three were ways of living in a community separated (to a greater or lesser extent) from ordinary lay life in the world around them. This fact stands out even more clearly when we remember that the communities were of men only, or of women only—they always consisted of vowed members of celibate groups.

This doesn't mean that dedicated lay Christians did not choose to live "poorly" in the world at every stage in our history. Without any doubt, experiments of that sort never abated, but their influence on the course of events was necessarily less effective. The surrounding world all too easily ignores, or takes for granted, or soon forgets the witness of remarkable individuals in their midst. But those who manage to create an organized support group or community may hope to make a real impact down the generations.

All three of the communities I've mentioned have definite advantages to recommend them to our attention, as well as shortcomings that must give us pause. But it is my conviction that their historical emergence was provoked by new cultural events, new challenges to the faith. Accordingly, I shall try to describe each of the three as creative responses to actual economic situations confronting the Church when they first arose.

The key notion I am proposing here is that, if it is to be rightly understood, each form of freely chosen Christian poverty must in its historical moment be related to the economic situation of its own day. It can't be grasped outside that context, for it will necessarily be a distinct answer to a specific economic challenge. If this contextual aspect of "poverty" is clarified, it may help us to see what may be needed in the rather different economic situation we are facing today.

Monastic Poverty

From at least the fifth to the eleventh centuries A.D. waves of mostly violent immigration flowed into the Western parts of the Roman Empire from the Eurasian steppes. This meant that during all those centuries "feudal disorder" became the dominant reality in what was later called Europe. Much of the civilized way of life of the old Empire was lost. Instead, brutal political and social conditions prevented commerce and enabled pillage, murders and local tyrannies nearly everywhere.

Although the monastic movement had started earlier in the Eastern parts of the Empire, in the West a monastery became an island of peace—an exceptional place of order and mutual respect, ruled firmly but kindly by abbot or abbess, where arts, crafts and learning could be cultivated by monks and nuns who shared a common life devoted to divine worship.

That, in a nutshell (oversimplified, of course) shows how monastic poverty was connected with its economic context. Outside the monastic walls we must recognize during those feudal centuries the disorders that plagued the lives of most Christians. Markets held mostly local produce. Commerce was unable to flow freely along the rivers or roads of Europe then. Bandits and brigands prevented any merchant from venturing forth with saleable goods. And ships could easily be pirated on sea or ocean everywhere.

As a result, people looked to the monasteries as the only places where Christian holiness could be seen. The world was under the dominion of Satan in a way that went beyond ordinary expectations. But in a monastery, to the extent that its goals were reached, the very opposite appeared: the Eucharist was celebrated at leisure and with dignity; the hours of the divine office were sung; fields were cultivated prayerfully; arts and crafts were practised; manuscripts were preserved, learning taught, libraries established and civilized traditions were handed down to the next generation. (Most of what we know today about the Classical ages was kept alive in the monasteries.)

If we look at those amazing foundations from an economic point of view, we see that they meant, not only individual simplicity of lifestyle, but common ownership of all monastic lands and goods. These were administered by the abbot or abbess with the help of their subordinate officers. Whenever this was well done, the monastic life presented a model to the surrounding world of a way of life in which justice, peace, mutual respect and charity prevailed. It was intended to be well-ordered (the image of Roman order was clearly preserved in the Rule of St. Benedict).

Now, a well-ordered life at home is exactly the meaning of "economy" in a community. In monastic poverty, then, a common life was put into actual practice by hundreds of thousands of men and women over many centuries. In their way of life together, material goods were carefully provided by the co-operation of all the members as means to a more important end, the worship of God at the centre of the community. If obedience to the abbot/abbess was given rather strong emphasis, that was because of the conditions of actual life in the world surrounding the monastery.

New members (young novices) had grown up in that disorderly world, were shaped by its miseries and vices, had received their call to Christian conversion amidst its crudities, and now needed to be firmly disciplined and re-formed by the teachings of Christ in the Gospel. St. Benedict wanted abbot and abbess to make sure that a remodelling of men and women candidates was actually brought about at an early stage of their spiritual formation.

Accordingly, they gave up all claims to personal ownership and devoted themselves instead to the common good of the monastery. Above all, they learned how to subordinate their work and their actual use of material goods to the higher end of divine service in a common life together.

These may seem like rather elementary virtues, but in a world where greed, rape and violence were a daily norm, the basics were taught in a monastic setting for a life of humble service that found its meaning and value in union with God and charity to every neighbour. Are we not beginning to search for ways of doing something similar today? Are greed, rape and violence not becoming more and more to be expected in our own world? How are we going to bring about a movement in the opposite direction?

However, the disadvantages of this kind of poverty soon showed themselves, too. While individual monks or nuns could be "poor" in the Christian sense, the monastery itself could too easily become wealthy. Can one really be a poor member of a rich community? Barons gave gifts, sought favours and influence, and claimed the right to name abbots and abbesses. Ordinary Christians in the world came bearing more gifts, seeking prayers for healing and longing for favours of every kind. As a result, the wealthier monasteries were soon enough plundered by barons or sacked by brigands.

In view of all this, the history of Western monasticism has been complicated by corruptions, dissolutions, and renewal movements of every imaginable sort: heroism and ignominy, achievements and blunders, holiness and villainy. The dominant tradition always managed to survive the worst disasters, but the problem of dealing with communal wealth seems never to have received an adequate solution during those early centuries.

Mendicant Poverty

By about the twelfth century in the West a dramatic growth of civilized institutions had begun to change the whole context of economic life. The waves of immigration had ended. A renewal of the whole Church was initiated by what is called "the Gregorian Reform"—a movement led by Pope Gregory VII and others to bring about radical changes in how the Church and society at large were to be organized. (This is too big a topic for me to treat here.)

Rivers and seas were opened to traffic. Trade and commerce began to flourish. Coined money was put into wide circulation for the first time. Goods were being produced for home and foreign consumption. Larger regions of public peace were gradually established and protected. Craft unions developed among towns and villages throughout Europe. Cathedrals were built, universities founded and a Christian art began to assert its distinctive powers.

Along with all this new wealth, of course, came dreadful corruptions right from the very start. But then a religious yearning to assert the values of Christian faith developed brand new experiments in poverty of spirit—especially, it should be noted, group experiments. Many of these were extremely radical, some quite wild and revolutionary—even violent in their own way. Most of them soon disappeared, but the Franciscan and Dominican friars and sisters managed to embody a new form of witness that has endured.

Friars differ from monks because they are not confined to a single location but move about from town to town, village to village, and live instead in "convents"—which in their original sense could be translated as "gathering places."

The friars spoke the common language of ordinary folk. They preached in churches or in the open, they listened to everyone's needs, gave counsel and the sacraments, worked and prayed. In a word, they made themselves available as humble witnesses to the real presence of the risen Christ wherever the new Christian civilization was being created.

How could the friars maintain their radical spirit and not be soon corrupted by the ever-greedy world in which they moved about? The answer seems to be that their spirituality was focused upon a new kind of Christian poverty.

To oversimplify again, we could say that the friars became the best witnesses to Christ amid a rich society. It was the rising wealth of Western Europe that triggered off a creative response and led to the new stress laid precisely on Christian poverty.

To put it briefly, they chose a voluntary poverty of alms-begging in order to turn well-off persons into "benefactors." In other words, their witness had to do with how the new wealth was to be used, what aims it was to seek, and whether it could become a means to the service of God in the world of daily life (and not merely in the monasteries).

Could the Church be effective amid the world then aborning? Or was holiness to be confined within monastic precincts? The fact that St. Francis of Assisi was seen in his lifetime as a sort of "Christ-figure living in the world" proves how successful this new witness to Christian poverty soon became. His immense popularity is shown by the rapid growth of the Franciscan Order.

And the communal dimension of Francis' ministry needs more attention here. St. Francis was quite reluctant to draw up a "rule" or set down in writing any elaborate constitutions. He preferred to use the Gospels as his sole witness to a Christian way of life, and he wanted to re-enact the sayings of Jesus in as literal a fashion as he could devise. While this attractive element of spontaneity in his spiritual witness to his times should not be discounted, it does to a certain extent distract our attention from his real remodelling of community life.

Even before the time of St. Francis, an intense longing to imitate the model of faith community given by Jesus and his little circle of "travelling disciples" in first-century Palestine had taken a strong hold over the feelings of devout believers. This image of Christian community was given the name vita apostolica, or "the way of life of the apostles" who had been chosen by Jesus to accompany him as he moved about Israel.

For our purposes here I draw attention to two false assumptions concerning this New Testament model (which may be influential with many Christians today). Both of these were mentioned in the last chapter: the "travelling disciples" of Jesus were thought to be spiritually more advanced than disciples who remained at home; and "giving away all one's possessions" in order to live by begging alms or by occasional service of others was taken to be the only authentic way to follow Jesus.

Since it is my conviction that these two assumptions are a continual source of confusion in our attempts to practise poverty today, they call for at least a brief discussion at this point. The vita apostolica was taken to be the ideal for everyone, the norm or standard for all Christians in every age. And in the thirteenth century, the first "age of the friars," St. Francis was seen to embody that model in a truly memorable way.

Francis's father was a rich merchant, and to escape his father's efforts to control him, he gave everything away, surrendered all claims, and even handed over his clothing so as to be entirely free! No doubt, he took the words of Jesus in the Gospel in a literal sense to mean precisely that: strip everything off, live without any secure income—just as Jesus and his little band of disciples did as they moved about Palestine in the first century. For their extremely simple needs they relied on alms or on gifts for work done. (They also did not concern themselves, it should be noted, about supporting wife and children.)

But did St. Francis expect all other Christians to follow this pattern as the only "correct" one for real Christians? The answer now given by scholars is "No, he did not." He saw it as a special vocation, a call from God that was exceptional, not a model for others to follow—or to feel guilty about not following.

It was a special form of witness to what the Gospel meant for others: to use their riches (money, possessions, homes, talents and opportunities) in the service of the Lord's kingdom in this world. For the risen Christ is present among us now, and his presence calls all of us who believe in him to live in a different way than those who care nothing for his teaching.

Francis understood this, we are told, but later times slipped into the old prejudice. Francis knew perfectly well that if most believers did as he did, there would be no one to beg from—the very idea is ridiculous. But down the centuries the bias in favour of "living by begging in the streets" as the only true image of what Jesus meant when he spoke of "poverty" has persisted with amazing tenacity. (Is it perhaps a perverse form of cop-out? It helps us to avoid actually having to live the Gospel if we interpret Jesus' central teaching as an "impossible ideal.")

The goal of Christian poverty gave St. Francis and his "little brothers" and "little sisters" the very practical purpose of putting the new wealth of Christian Europe to work in building a new kind of society. This was to be a community that believed in divine reality in their midst—in their very union as the Body of Christ risen. The radical witness of poverty was meant to liberate those who believed from their enslavement to riches and enable them to construct by divine grace what came to be called "Christendom."

Despite its historical weaknesses, which were considerable, this was a remarkable new event in human history. The cathedrals were its main symbol, but consider a few of its other contributions: the public peace of cities, parliaments, trade and craft guilds, universities, and all the Western arts (architecture, painting, drama, sculpture, music, and so on). This great cultural explosion was celebrated for us in Kenneth Clark's wonderful television series, simply called "Civilization" (1969). European culture, from which has come the modern technology and science now transforming the whole world, was born at this time.

Is Christian poverty as influential as this? I think the answer is Yes—even though it must be seen together with many other factors. But further signs of its remarkable powers probably lie before us in the future. For when embraced in a radical way by persons in large numbers, it can unleash unexpected acts of creativity in human societies.

The shortcomings of mendicant poverty, however, need a brief mention as well. Besides the misunderstandings already noted above, there are the difficulties of "withdrawal and return," as they may be called. By this I mean that a small, exceptional group of witnesses are required (if my analysis is correct) to inspire the large number of well-off believers to become benefactors of the common good. But how shall the special witnesses (the brothers or sisters) remain true to their calling? How can they possibly avoid becoming victims themselves to the drive for riches?

The historical answer given to that question was: by withdrawing from the world for a time in order to build up a capital of spiritual resources, which could then be invested in society during a time of re-entry into human affairs. In short, there are two different times implied by mendicant poverty. There is the time of withdrawal into convents (for spiritual deepening and heightening—the vertical dimension) and there is also the time of return to the horizontal world of secular busy-ness, when the resources amassed at the convent soon become "spent."

This familiar arrangement (we do the same for health reasons when we take a holiday) includes a number of difficulties for the Church as a whole. Even when it works well for the "special vocation" people, what about the vast number of believers living in the world? Do they not tend to be seen as second-class Christians? Setting that aside, we should ask how ordinary Christians might be able to renew their spiritual lives and to sustain themselves in their devotion to service of God's kingdom amid the usual egotism, tyrannies and malign influences of human life in the world.

The development by the later Middle Ages of small houses of "retreat" for lay persons was a sign of this urgent need. Just as the monasteries became hospitable to lay sojourners in search of silence and prayer, so the mendicant convents began to set aside rooms or to devise special places of "recollection" for devout lay followers and "Third Order" members. But, it must be said, this effort could only touch the tip of the iceberg. The ongoing evils of so-called Christian nations in Europe are proof enough of that fact. And even if many individuals could be renewed and revitalized, deplorable problems of a social and communal kind could not be handled in that way.

Active Poverty

By the sixteenth century a whole range of new forces had developed in Europe, forces which were beginning to move economic activity in quite a different direction. For Christians still nourished by the spiritual resources of the medieval world, the main obstacles now to be faced were "vested interests." By this I mean not just the growth of national monarchies (the rise of nationalism in Europe, the first great European nations in Spain, France and England), and the growing secular power of great families; much worse was the power of wealth in the Church itself.

Efforts to reform the Western Church had been called for and attempted on many sides for several centuries already—all to no avail, so far as its institutions were actually working. When the very bodies which are supposed to enact the measures of reform are themselves corrupted by wealth, no real action can be expected.

Words (even very eloquent words) will be spoken, of course. Lengthy documents (even very well-aimed documents) will be drawn up. Decrees will be passed. Assurances will be given. But no effective changes will be made because exceptions and evasions will be included in every pretended measure of reform. And so the Protestant Reformation came into being— outside the institutions of the old Church.

The situation of the Church had changed in a number of ways. Printing presses had been invented by Gutenberg (putting the Scriptures into everyone's hands). The American continent had been discovered; in fact, global explorations were underway (opening up vistas of gold and silver mines). The Italian Renaissance was spreading throughout Europe (providing new interest in Classical models for every aspect of culture). And in political life the older scheme of a unified "Christendom" was giving way to the independent national monarchies already noted. In fact, massive change was in the air, not the least of which was a new sense of individualism (the beginnings of modern individualism).

Ignatius of Loyola belonged to the same age as Copernicus—but so did Luther and Calvin. Perhaps we can put brackets around the serious differences between these religious leaders, differences which seemed of supreme importance during the last few centuries but which today (when the separated churches are coming together at last) we may "downsize" a little. Or, to change the image, perhaps we could put their fierce controversies onto the back burner so as to focus, up front, on the ways in which they resemble one another.

One remarkable similarity is their relentless drive to real action in this world. Luther wanted to separate the realms of faith and of secular activity so as to enable them to work more effectively together. Calvin firmly united the two realms in an effort to bring into being an efficiently governed city of God. Ignatius sought the renewal of Church-committed members from below and from within (their spirituality)—so that action-oriented persons might serve the glory of God in the world.

That common trait unites all the reformers, both Catholic and Protestant, in efforts focused on changing the actual lives of Christian people. Not that they abandoned their concern for heaven and hell. But they gave their main attention to this-worldly action in order that everyone's eternal destiny might be assured. That shift of emphasis was called for by the times in which they lived. And it makes a big difference in the matter of poverty.

How people use goods in this world was becoming more important than whether the goods should or should not be given away. For Ignatius Loyola, at least, how decisions were to be made about possessions was becoming more crucial than what the decisions might actually be. When deciding, are we serving ourselves, or Satan, or are we serving the will of God? And how can we find the spiritual freedom to choose well between good options during our lifetime?

St. Ignatius never worked out an elaborate theory of Christian poverty, but in practice he gave us new ways to become "poor in action." In other words, I think his active spirituality included a form of active poverty (in the Christian sense of the term). This may be summed up in three key features of his teaching. First, he insisted on a radical purification from disordered attachment to riches (meaning the craving for possessions) as well as to honours (positions, acclaim, success). Secondly, when deciding how to use wealth, talents, educational advantages (every sort of "goods"), he required a willingness to notice, and to respond to, divine initiatives felt in the heart. Thirdly, he expected all Catholics to commit themselves intensely and faithfully to the Church's teaching and guidance (the faith community to which they belonged).

In this context Christian poverty refers to the flexible use of all available goods as means to achieve the greater religious ends to which the members of the community are committed. The same context includes a sense of struggle against evil forces in the world (we find this, too, in Luther and Calvin).

The human world that is the scene for the Christian drama presents antagonism, obstacles, sudden bursts of action, new decisions to be faced in new situations, and so on. Yet most important of all is reliance on the presence of Jesus to his followers. He is always sending the Spirit to them, consoling them, and leading them through ever new difficulties to the greater glory of God.

The advantages of this notion of Christian poverty are so obvious that we don't need to dwell on them. But the drawbacks do call for some attention. In the sixteenth century there was as yet no awareness of human institutions as anything but "sacred"—even in politics, as Shakespeare's plays reveal. As a result, active poverty says nothing about changing sinful social structures or recognizing human responsibility for badly designed institutions. Many disagreed about what structures God wanted and accused their opponents of getting this wrong, but they all agreed that their social structures were divine in origin.

Until the secular realm could develop a great deal further—enough to bring about awareness of our own responsibility in devising the institutions that shape our way of life—active poverty remained limited to working within the structures as given. That, as we now know, is a severe restriction. And we are forced to admit that it refers as well to much of what passes for "divine" in the institutions of the Church itself—a thorny matter indeed.

This brief and oversimplified review of major developments in our spiritual tradition will have to do for our purposes here. It refers solely to ways in which Christian poverty has been understood and put into practice by three great spiritual communities, and it attempts to describe the economic contexts that provoked the different responses mentioned.

As an historical effort, I realize that what I have said leaves much to be desired. But at least it may raise questions for us today in more specific forms. What do we see as new and unusual in our own economic context? And if we can gain some insight into that issue, then how might the Gospel teachings on Christian poverty be realized in our new situation? Those are the questions to be addressed in the next two chapters.

4

What Is Special About Our Economic Situation?

The last few centuries have seen the emergence of modern sciences alongside remarkable developments in mechanics. Then came the Industrial Revolution, the "Enlightenment" of the eighteenth century, followed by the French Revolution, and the gradual influence of modern technologies upon most of our social institutions.

Since all those events have remarkably transformed our ways of living in this world, it should be perfectly clear that the medieval system of economic life no longer exists. The whole context has changed once again. And it follows that our notions of Christian poverty will need to be renewed in quite a fundamental way. We can't simply apply earlier "solutions" to the new situation in which we find ourselves.

Obviously, "Christendom" is no more. It is possible to regret this, and some do. But it is also possible to see the passing of medieval ways as the will of God and for our good. In any case, the Industrial Revolution (which began about 1750 in

Britain and later spread through all the Western nations) is certainly one of the greatest changes in all human history. Despite the sufferings that its advent has brought upon many persons, and despite any false philosophies which may have attended it, its claim on our attention remains—if only because of the enormity of its impact.

It seems to me that huge transformations of this sort ought to be seen as coming somehow under the rule of divine providence. Our greed and merciless behaviour during every change in human affairs can never eliminate the divine striving for our good. The profound insight that "God writes straight through crooked lines" can be seen in economic changes, too.

Today even in China (an immense nation, long isolated from the rest of the earth) the leaders boast of the progress they are making in "modernization"—a Western term. In plain fact the entire planet is now bound together economically, whether for better or for worse. No country can expect to cut itself off from the rest of the world and simply "cultivate its own garden." That, we know, would only lead to disaster.

Agricultural Economy

The way most pre-modern societies lived—despite all the variations and new developments down the ages—may be summed up under the word "agricultural." This simply points to the fact that the ongoing ways of providing food, clothing and other human necessities (shelter, means of travel and communication) mainly depended on intensive efforts at farming.

Of course, hunting and fishing continued in most societies. But a very large portion of the population was kept busy in cultivating the fields. Traditional methods were employed for ages and ages. Sometimes improved techniques were discovered (better plows, rotation of crops, new grains, domestication of animals, and so on), but literally for thousands of years human civilization continued to be agriculturally based.

It hadn't always been so. In what are called "tribal" cultures (and even today there are societies continuing to live a tribal, even nomadic, life to some extent), the economy was based mainly on hunting, fishing and fruit-gathering. Nature did most of the work—without much human cultivation. Perhaps some rudimentary sowing of fields was undertaken, but when growth diminished, the tribes tended to move to somewhere else. Their hunting stock often moved, too, or appeared seasonally in other regions, so in any case they had to leave the fields.

It's likely that for the longest stretches of human history (hundreds of thousands of years) the economy was simply tribal—meaning quite undeveloped. We shouldn't glamorize the life of our ancestors, but we could say generally that there was very little difference between rich and poor in most tribal societies. For the most part, everyone was expected to participate in most kinds of work and to share in what the hunters and gatherers obtained. And when they moved, all the members—according to their abilities—shouldered the few common possessions.

But when new methods of farming were developed along great river-systems (for example, the Tigris and Euphrates in Sumeria, the Nile in Egypt, the Indus in India, the Yangtze in China), new kinds of civilization began to multiply. Ditches and canals and dams brought life-giving waters to more and more fields.

This meant that larger numbers of peasants learned how to prepare the earth, to sow and to harvest a wider variety of crops. Tribal societies—like the ancient Hebrews—tended to be subordinated to the powerful new empires along the great rivers. Agriculturally based civilizations brought such immense benefits to human beings that the main transition from tribal to agricultural economies was never in serious doubt.

Some scholars claim that this was the most far-reaching and significant change in all of human history. Writing—the alphabet—appeared, along with education, planning for the future ("fat years" followed by "lean years"), various social grades, organization of political activities, development of arts and crafts, and so on.

But it also brought many great evils, especially the distressing contrast between rich and poor, the powerful few and the powerless many—a sense of injustice and the desire for wealth. In their wake came a sea of troubles: oppression and murder, piracy, kidnapping for ransom, pride of place and the arrogance of power, not to mention increasing taxation and exorbitant prices. Wherever human beings organized a more complex way of life, some members would unfailingly find clever ways of exploiting those who were naive or unprotected.

Jesus himself grew up, lived and preached his message of God's kingdom against the background of an agricultural economy. His parables incidentally reveal the various aspects of rural life. In fact, the whole Bible is filled with imagery borrowed from that kind of social environment. And, as we have seen, our great religious orders developed their differing lifestyles in succeeding phases of agricultural society.

In short, all our spiritual principles on the subject of Christian poverty gained their first expression in language that is deeply embedded in pre-modern economic arrangements. Nothing else, of course, would have been intelligible in those ages. But this means that our situation today adds up to a change in the whole system—not merely to a few cosmetic adjustments that could leave the former system intact. And so it calls, I believe, for quite a different response on our part.

Industrial Economy

To see what Christian poverty may come to mean in our new situation, I'll begin by mentioning three special features of the industrial economy: first, its secular quality (in contrast to the medieval sense of sacred institutions); secondly, its abundance (versus the traditional scarcity of goods); thirdly, its orientation towards future development here on earth (rather than to eternal, other-worldly goals).

Next, I want to distinguish two components or stages in Christian poverty (this difference, not usually noticed in the Middle Ages, will enable us to deal more wisely with the excessive stress experienced today): the first component consists in grasping the special challenge to faith arising from each economic situation; the second refers to a creative faith-response aimed at that challenge.

After showing why this two-stage approach is scarcely visible in the traditional, agricultural understanding of Christian poverty, I will focus my discussion on our current economic arrangements. First, how do these secular pressures afflict us today? Secondly, how might we give a more effective response in faith to this new kind of challenge? My answer to the latter question will remain at a general level, but in the last chapter I will look at more concrete ways of putting it into practice.

The foremost feature of our present economic situation is its secularity, I think. Our financial system and our technological production of goods are known (understood and felt in practice) to be devised by human beings. None of its concrete workings were "given to us by God" as part of the eternal nature of things. At least, that's not how we feel about it.

In the past most peoples took it for granted that their way of life (including their economic arrangements) had been designed by divine powers and belonged to the very structure of reality. They told sacred stories about how their gods or semi-divine ancestors had invented those ways and handed them down to all generations.

Even our medieval Christian forebears assumed that their economy was God's will for them. Like their political and social institutions (kingship and aristocracy, merchant and peasant classes), their financial institutions were sacred for them and thought to be unchangeable in their main forms of operation.

But most of us today don't experience our work, our banking and use of credit cards, our stores and cars and shopping trips as divinely ordered activities! Not in the least. They have become possible, we know, through the technical expertise of human beings. Besides, if humanly devised, it follows that our economic system and all its processes can be changed.

And they are always in process of change—much more quickly than we usually want. Because we feel them all to be so entirely secular, then, our economic ways (our ways of earning our living) are at the root of our worst feelings of insecurity—despite the fact that we are better off in so many ways than people of earlier centuries. The heightened stressfulness of our humanly devised, and therefore our rapidly changing society arises directly from this secular feeling. Earlier times did not experience such burdens as acutely as so many people do in our world.

The Affluent Society

A second major feature of modern economic arrangements, of course, has to do with abundance, and this makes a big impact on our sense of what Christian poverty might mean today. The "affluent society" is all around us, even if we experience "hard times" and mostly feel the strain and struggle of trying to find enough income to keep up or even to get by on less than before.

Let's look at this factor a little more closely. What I am referring to is the production and availability of goods and services that were missing for most members of all former societies—and for many other parts of the world today. In earlier centuries even kings, queens and those close to them could not simply turn on a tap and expect to run hot water over their fingers (but we take this for granted), or take a shower at a moment's notice (as we usually expect to do).

Central heating in our homes, soft fabrics to clothe our bodies, a wide choice of foods to eat, rapid means of travel and transportation (compared with the slow means of former centuries) and fingertip modes of instant communication—this list could go on and on, as we know (films, concerts, headsets, videos, news, pills, hospitals, dental work . . .).

Today, in other words, we feel the burden of hard times against the background of all this abundance. Those who lived in earlier times (and many people from other parts of the world at present), if they could drop in on us right now, would perhaps ask what we could be complaining about—they'd be glad to have our kind of trouble. True enough, but it misses the point, I think.

Once modern goods abound, in other words, once the overall standard of living has been raised in a given society, then its members begin to experience a new kind of stress that goes along with it. And when the whole situation has become secular in its feeling (drained of religious meaning and value), then the insecurities felt in an ongoing way—in the background day by day—are increased to a level that causes new kinds of bodily illness: heart attacks, cancer, and so on. We are quite familiar with the immense increase of "stress-related diseases" that belong in a special way to our time.

But let's look at the whole modern picture from a different angle. In the Middle Ages it was taken for granted that "usury"—meaning, lending money for interest—was a grave sin. But today our entire economic system depends on lending money for the interest that may be gained from it. In fact, higher or lower interest rates are an important concern of every modern government—with good reason, since the day-to-day welfare of many citizens depends on it.

Why is there such a big difference in medieval and modern economies? Well, without going into technical explanations, a huge shift has taken place in the underlying system itself. In medieval times this meant that individuals who borrowed at interest (persons other than heads of government) usually had no way of paying back the sum borrowed. Their forms of industry were not "productive" of increased profits, as ours are expected to be.

By straining hard they might have been able to pay the interest, but not to repay the capital borrowed. As a result, by borrowing a large sum they had become enslaved to another person's income—for the rest of their lives. The Church condemned usury because it often caused financial enslavement in the circumstances of that time.

It's better, then, to define "usury" by including the economic arrangements which made it so evil in its context. When taken out of that situation, "lending at interest" no longer has the same meaning. But "loan-sharking," or lending at extravagant levels of interest to people in desperate need, might be seen as our modern equivalent of the medieval sin.

Our situation today is usually quite different. The Industrial Revolution depended on large concentrations of wealth (not just money, but land, power sources, giant factories, natural resources, machinery, salaried workers, distribution systems, sales outlets, and so on). In order to make this work, large sums of money have to be called upon continually, and that means borrowing at interest.

The whole system depends on investment of capital of all kinds: purchasing raw materials, producing new goods, competing for markets, making profits or sustaining losses, training workers and managers, and so forth. By the time a wholesale change of this sort had taken place in modern economies, the medieval notion of usury no longer applied. The Church withdrew its condemnation (or let it fall silent) because the whole system had been altered in a fundamental way.

The same must be said for our spiritual attitudes. We do not live in an economy of want but in an economy of abundance. The idea that "Christian poverty" means that all those who believe in Jesus Christ should refrain from owning modern products or never lend or borrow money at interest is obviously wide of the mark.

In fact, anyone continuing to hold such a view is not dealing with the actual world that confronts us. And so it follows that, since our spirituality needs to make sense within the economic context of our own time, it will have to take new forms and find a better language.

But many assumptions about Christian poverty were developed in the very different financial situations of former centuries and have simply not been updated by those who continue to make those assumptions today. In a sense, this essay seeks to stimulate fresh thinking on this topic by people who may not have given the matter much thought before—may not have examined their reasons for holding the views in question.

A first step in this direction might be an invitation to appreciate the efforts of good economists, effective businessmen, and shrewd entrepreneurs. Surely our spiritual response, so far from running down those activities, ought to include gratitude and appreciation for them. We ought to praise them whenever they are well and honestly done. A well-ordered economic system is essential to our common welfare and calls for everyone's cooperation.

If this sounds too obvious a truth to require emphasis, I would reply that I have encountered far too many short-sighted appeals to pre-modern ways—in the name of Christian poverty. Are the only "real" Christians those who remain wedded to pre-modern cultural views?

If we own or make use of automobiles, are we being untrue to the Gospel? It would be hard to argue that way openly, but I find too many people who seem somehow to take it for granted. It's true enough that some individuals today are called to special vocations, to identify their lives with those "left out" of the abundant society and to bring a real witness to deplorable conditions in many parts of the world.

But special vocations of this kind are exceptional. They cannot exemplify the main form of Christian poverty for us who live amid highly developed economies. All the same, they do provide an important service. They become a living witness to the serious shortcomings of our current system. They remind us that what is going on in our society is not good enough. This fact is still true in our time and binds us to the company of Christians in every former century.

Though our highly developed economies tend to produce an abundance, even superfluity of consumer goods, often to our own surprise we find ourselves under heavy pressures. There are so many choices to make, so much doubt about what we've already decided, and far too much difficulty in making and in keeping any long-term commitments. This is a new kind of stress, Karl Rahner points out, and more burdensome than the tensions felt in former times.

Our Sense Of A Journey

A third key feature of our present situation concerns our forward thrust in time, our tendency to expect new models to appear on the market and (although we are learning to be more cautious) to hope they will be better than the former models. To put it simply, modern culture is more focused on the future than on the past.

In medieval times people tended to think that any changes introduced would be for the worse. Christians took it for granted that the end of the world would be preceded by many severe disruptions. Only after a great deal of suffering on earth would the Lord appear to set all to rights and establish the final kingdom. In the meantime, the day-by-day forward movement of time was not seen as very meaningful or valuable in itself.

At least in material matters, people today have formed the opposite expectation. Since we are collectively responsible for putting together the technical arrangements which we enjoy or which trouble us, we also hope for future improvements. If they are not in fact forthcoming, we look around for someone to blame for this.

We can easily work up a lot of resentment if our economic situation is not better than it used to be, or if we've fallen upon hard times. Things are supposed to get better, not worse—we take that to be a "normal" attitude (though it's quite a recent development for human beings, in point of fact).

At Vatican Council II one of the symbols of the Church put forward with new emphasis was that of "the Pilgrim People." This was not a new phrase, of course, but it took on a new sense in the modern age because of the attitude I have just mentioned.

Perhaps our expectations (in the advanced nations) about material improvements will have to be cut back considerably—in view of the world-wide needs of all the other nations. Our level of consuming goods is far too high in comparison with theirs. But setting that aside for the moment (we'll get back to it later), we can surely see that we should look forward to spiritual improvements in the future.

For a pilgrim is seeking a holy place on the road ahead. And in this sense believers today are hoping for new developments in this world—not only when we reach the life beyond death. But our spiritual expectations must be based (among other things) on realistic financial arrangements. What this means is that our Christian poverty must include the striving for better (more just and more personally respectful) economic structures on earth, beginning with our own society—where we live.

It's not difficult to see how stressful this striving for social justice can be for believers today. We must seek to bring about changes not only in global institutions, but also amidst our own situations in the city where we live. In fact, we are obliged almost daily to face difficult questions about our own financial arrangements. It's not a simple matter to adapt to all this.

Two Components In Christian Poverty

Without trying to be complete, I have devoted a few pages above to some of the more remarkable features of our own situation today. What I want to focus upon now is what I take to be the key issue in any attempt to update our sense of Christian poverty—namely, the special kind of stress which we experience in making our financial arrangements.

How do we moderns differ in this from our medieval ancestors? And how might this difference, if we can express it properly, affect our way of practising the virtue of Christian poverty, as Jesus our Lord recommended it to us in the Gospel?

In my judgment, it helps to notice that there are always two components which are combined in the notion of Christian poverty —not just one. The first component is the specific stress experienced in the economic dimension. The second component is the response of Christian faith to that economic stress.

In other words, we begin from a definite cultural context which always places a distressing burden on the backs of the population in question, especially on the "little" members of that people (the less well-placed, the less skilled or clever, the disadvantaged). We begin, that is, with "Satan's dominion," where the powers of darkness are at work. No one should be surprised at this common human reality since it is one aspect of the state of "original sin" into which we are all born.

But Christian faith calls forth, from all those who believe, a basic response to the facts in question (this is the second component). In the case of the Western monks, as we have seen, the response was to create islands of order amidst the seas of economic and social disorder which surrounded them. That was not a final solution to human problems, but it was a meaningful response of faith to a distressing historical situation of that age.

Our faith requires that we make a spiritual choice. It must take on a definite character responding to the actual circumstances of our time. But in every case the spiritual choice we make individually and as a group ought to arise from an interiorly graced reordering of the human spirit, a new attitude. This is what I believe is intended by the words spoken by Jesus when he opened his public ministry: "Be converted (change your whole attitude)! And believe the good news: the kingdom of God is at hand!" (Mark 1:15).

Our change of attitude refers to a whole range of other important dimensions of life as well, but it certainly includes the material arrangement of life, on which so much depends. I have tried to show in earlier chapters that Jesus is definite and explicit on this point, and that succeeding centuries of Christians have agreed unanimously.

The real questions have to do with the precise nature of the demands which we face today (the first component), and the special kind of choice we are called upon to make in our rather different economic situation (the second component).

Physical Destitution

What has blocked too many minds from answering these questions clearly, I believe, has been the very success of the medieval response. That medieval success still keeps its hold on our minds and hearts—even though we may all agree in general that our modern economy has a very different basis, namely an industrial and technological one, which has entirely overthrown the agriculturally based economy of the Middle Ages.

Now, the key to the medieval answer was to identify the term "poverty" with what I may call physical destitution. That made a lot of sense in medieval conditions. In agricultural economies people faced a daily threat of "destitution," meaning the danger of not finding sufficient resources for food, shelter, clothing, and so forth, on a continuing basis. Many members of society lived so close to deprivation that any change or accident (such as a flood or drought) could put their lives in severe crisis. Short of any crisis, there was the difficulty of having to put the greatest part of one's energies from day to day into the effort of mere survival. That is what I mean by this phrase.

The term "destitution," then, is meant to cover a wide range of physically insecure situations in life, from difficult drudgery every day at one end of the scale, all the way to acute hunger, cold and fear (for myself and for those who may depend on me) at the other end. I am adding the word "physical" to bring out the life-threatening aspects of that experience.

As soon as we begin to think of poverty in these terms, we realize how present it is in our own world. Of the more than four billion human beings now living on earth, we are told that about one fourth, or nearly one billion of them, are in actual "physical destitution" or near to it most of the time!

In this sense, "poverty" is an evil. Things ought not to be this way. From the viewpoint of the resources and technology of our modern production and distribution systems, we have the actual means of overcoming these terrible threats. And I'm referring to long-term, systematic solutions—not merely to emergency relief efforts.

Why, then, does grinding poverty of this kind (in the sense of physical destitution) continue to plague the earth and bother our consciences in the more developed regions? The short answer would have to address the issues of social justice and injustice, of self-interested groups protecting positions of privilege, of the slow and slight growth in awareness of what is involved, and so on—this question was addressed in my opening chapter.

But right here I want to emphasize the two different senses of the term "poverty" which emerge from these facts. Poverty as physical destitution is an evil that ought to be overcome. Christian poverty, on the other hand, is a virtue based on the teachings of Jesus in the Gospel and urged upon us in our spiritual tradition down all the centuries to our own time.

Now, these two meanings could be brought together fairly closely as long as agriculturally based economies provided the environment for Christian life. That is, until the end of the Middle Ages the witness given by radical Christians to evangelical poverty could take the form of a freely chosen lifestyle of physical destitution.

What this signified was that a few exceptional persons (who began with better means at their disposal) freely chose because of religious motives to live in physical destitution. They did this in order to bring to the attention of others their need to use their God-given possessions in the worship of God and the service of God and others.

St. Francis, whose father was a wealthy merchant, began by interesting others in repairing broken-down churches. When his father complained and called him to "normal" behaviour, Francis handed over all his possessions (even his clothing) to signify the choice he felt called (exceptionally) by God to make. He wanted to live quite literally in physical destitution.

St. Ignatius Loyola, although a member of the aristocracy, was inspired to live for some years in the most radical kind of physical destitution as a sign to believers who could appreciate his point: union with Christ called everyone to a total change of attitude in their use of wealth on earth—in marriage arrangements, for example, or in receiving or disposing of benefices in the Church. (His name for this radical choice in his little book, the Spiritual Exercises, was "actual poverty.")

This notion was acceptable enough in an agriculturally based economy. And why could this be so? Because physical destitution was not at that time looked upon as an evil to be eradicated but was generally accepted, at least in its less severe forms, as the lot of many people. Of course, alms were given by "benefactors" to the poor because that was how the system worked. But there was no question then of trying to change the system itself.

As a result, physical destitution could be freely chosen as a clear sign of Christian poverty. The two different notions could be referred to by the same term: both could be called "poverty" without further explanation.

At that time the first component of Christian poverty (the specific stress experienced in the economic dimension) was the sort of hardship I've been calling "physical destitution." Some forms of this might today be called "grinding poverty," but the range and degree of impoverishment is considerable.

It always amazes us as Westerners to discover how many persons living in physical destitution of various kinds can still lead happy lives and be so generous to one another, even being willing to share the little food they have. Perhaps it means that, despite the burdens of their life, they are culturally well-developed in the second component—the spiritual choice to respond unselfishly to their situation in life.

All the same, we should not be blind to the fact that not all members of those societies feel the same way. As knowledge of new possibilities spreads to them, many people become angry and resentful at their lot—it isn't their own fault, nor is it God's decision. Rather, it involves a good deal of human oppression!

Besides, to accept physical destitution too readily means to support it—even to co-operate in its continuance. In the nineteenth century Karl Marx put his finger on this new understanding: religion, he said, could easily become "the opium of the people," something that kept the poor masses quiet during their exploitation by a tiny elite.

But in the pre-modern societies of our Western or medieval culture such notions of social injustice were quite inconceivable to most people. No way of changing social structures for the better could enter their minds. And so the physical destitution of many members of each society could be experienced simply as their given place in life (first component). Those who believed intensely in God's saving love could then respond to it with detachment and trust (second component).

Christian poverty could be seen at that time (without further question) as the choice of, or readiness to accept, physical destitution because one was graced to place one's whole security in God alone. How it might work out in practice would be different for persons variously placed in life. For many, this would mean accepting their lot; for a few, it would signify leaving wealth and honours in order to bring a special witness to the world.

That graced choice (not everyone obtained it) could replace the all-too-human tendency to make the desire for riches dominant in one's life. A frustrated desire for riches could easily lead to miserliness, or to fatalism, chronic fear, bitterness of heart, and many other vices. Christian poverty in medieval conditions enabled believers in Christ to gain a radical trust in God. A deep sense of this virtue has become part and parcel of our spiritual tradition, even though times have changed so much since then that the question must be asked anew: how in our different circumstances today might it be put into practice?

Modern Consumerism
And Addiction

If physical destitution is the key for understanding what Christian poverty meant in the Middle Ages of Western culture, it can no longer serve that purpose today. In agricultural economies a shortage of necessary goods was taken for granted. But in our modern economy of abundance, physical destitution is clearly seen to be an evil which ought to be eradicated—not only in the advanced nations, but everywhere in the world. We are not there yet by a long shot, but that is where we should be heading. The result is that we can no longer use "physical destitution" as our model for the virtue of Christian poverty.

That does not mean, of course, that what Jesus recommends in the Gospel is no longer relevant to us. Rather, it means that we must make a serious effort to disengage our minds from the merely agricultural elements bound into our traditional teaching. Then we could rethink the meaning and value of what our Lord teaches. We might be able to realize it more effectively in our own cultural situation. My suggestion, as a way of getting started, is to take "consumerism and addiction" as a key to our present economic experience.

Our secular, affluent culture, I have been arguing, always brings with it an undercurrent of distress and compulsion. Because our technological society is known to be humanly devised, not given by God, the stress-level is greatly enhanced. We can't escape responsibility, for we are part of the whole system. And yet it tends to overwhelm us. Nothing reveals this so well as do consumerism and addiction.

These are not new ideas in themselves—I assume that all my readers are familiar enough with them. Consumerism does not refer only to buying and using up "commodities" (food, clothing, utensils, furniture, and so on, which have been produced or prepared for our use). No one can live in our world today without consuming goods. No, it becomes an "ism" when it tends to dominate our sense of who we are.

Instead of remaining means to higher ends, material goods become the main goal of life when consumerism takes over. Then our spiritual substance is entirely devoted to acquiring and consuming what is for sale in the stores. It's no secret that many members of our Western societies (perhaps the majority of them?) fall under the grip of consumerism to one degree or other.

An additional fact to remember about consumerism is that it exerts a mounting pressure on its victims, a relentless drive. Old models have to be thrown away, not only because they are beginning to fall apart, but also because the new models are so enticing. And this repeats itself every year, every season. What we already own seems paltry compared with what we'd like to buy, or feel we must obtain.

Furthermore, our level of income is too low for what we now consider to be "necessities." We are already indebted beyond our actual means—slowly we realize to what extent we have become enslaved to monthly payments that are more than we can bear.

This consumerism, it seems clear, has become the modern form of the "desire for riches" found also in agricultural societies. Where medieval people imagined the devil tempting them all the time to fall into sin, in our modern situation we are continually incited by commercials to seek more commodities.

Our slickly produced ads tempt us on all sides by appealing to our pride, covetousness, lust, anger, gluttony, envy and sloth. Just because it is done with jingles and humour (as well as with the "hard sell"), this does not mean that it isn't a serious pressure—although we are too secular-minded to see the devil in it. In fact, consumerism has invaded the hearts of modern people to a degree we don't often recognize.

I have added a second term, "addiction," even though its meaning might have been included under the first. My motive is to bring out explicitly the damaging side of our economic processes in the spiritual realm. Some might prefer to mention toxic waste as endangering our natural environment, but here I want to emphasize the damage being done to our psyche—to the Western soul, to the human spirit—so noticeably in our century.

The false overemphasis given to technological goods in modern societies and the terrible effects this has on our culture can be clearly seen (among other signs) in our widespread tendency to addictions of many sorts. Tobacco, alcohol and drug addictions are the most obvious, and recently we have grown aware of how many friends and family members suffer from "co-dependency," that is, an indirect dependence on the addiction that has enslaved a person who is important to them.

These "big three" of substance abuse may eventually kill their main victims, but co-dependent in all addictions suffer from various degrees of psychic injury. And beyond such individual injuries, we notice, our modern economy brings severe pressures to bear on every form of traditional community, breaking down families and other natural associations. This leads to a fearful number of divorces, increased tensions between generations (parents and teens), and intensified loneliness, isolation and misunderstanding. The fact that we are so busy trying to find solutions for all these problems simply highlights the social damage involved.

Addictions may be taken as desperate efforts to avoid psychic distress (for example, extreme dieting in overly thin individuals or kleptomania by members of higher-income families). This kind of distress is not caused by ugly physical appearances or by any need for possessions, but seems to arise from the spiritual insecurity felt so intensely by individuals in modern societies.

Most basic of all, of course, because it underlies all the rest, is the drive to succeed in the rat race to gain more commodities. Success is usually measured in modern culture by levels of income. Sad to see, those addicted insist upon "conspicuous consumption," displaying to others the possessions purchased by that income. And aside from the sense of failure, or fear of it, which plagues the efforts of many, perhaps most, members of society, there is also the deeper suspicion of vanity in the project itself. Does a higher income really prove anything at all? What is the purpose of so much striving?

No one will be surprised if I say at this point that the special kinds of psychic stress deriving from consumerism and addiction have in recent decades introduced or triggered off a whole range of tension-related diseases. These are the typical illnesses of our time: strokes, heart failure, high blood pressure, stomach ulcers, colitis, cancer, chronic depression, and so on. What the high incidence of these diseases seems to be telling us is that we are suffering from much worse insecurity, much more intense stress, than our forebears did in agricultural societies.

Unemployment

I hope that what I have written above can account, to some degree of accuracy, for the first component of Christian poverty today—that is, for the specific kind of stress experienced in the economic dimension of our own time, the burden felt on our backs or the tension felt in our hearts because of the financial pressures threatening us as an ordinary part of our economic situation.

New developments in unemployment might bring this out even more clearly. Obviously, to be without a job means a severe loss of income and a fearful absence of meaning and value. Joblessness hits people in their family relationships, but it also affects their innermost sense of self-worth. It is never easy to respond well to unemployment in our society.

We are currently suffering through a recession in which plant closings, bankruptcies and severe cutbacks in labour have been throwing huge numbers of wage-earners out of work. But, worst of all, commentators keep telling us that the excessively high levels of joblessness across the land are not going to go away—even after our economy has recovered from the recession we have been experiencing.

In former times we were always reassured that economic recovery would lead to more jobs for everyone. Now we are being told to face the bleak prospect that very few new jobs will accompany the kind of recovery that is predicted. In other words, the huge number of jobs already lost will not return.

If this should be true, what will it do to us? What will become of the large percentage of our people presently unemployed? And what of all those who are already "underemployed"?—that is, working part-time, working for less than before, suffering from steeply decreased incomes? Pressures of this kind are building up the psychic stress on whole families dependent on wage-earners.

On another front, fisherfolk on the seacoasts are receiving wave after wave of bad news about their future. It seems likely that it has been "technological progress" in fish-gathering that has depleted the fish stocks we once thought to be limitless.

The same may be said of native peoples who have from time immemorial lived by hunting and trading pelts. Modern economies tend relentlessly to undermine their traditional way of life, and should they seek modern solutions to their needs, they find themselves inviting our stressful lifestyles, along with unemployment, into their unprepared societies.

The Second Component

If these insecurities do indeed (as I think) define the specific stressfulness of our modern economic situation (first component), then how might we in faith make a more effective response to the burdens of our world? This question, of course, expresses the second component of Christian poverty.

In order to give an adequate reply, it will not be enough to seek healing for the damage done to individuals. Rather, a new attitude is required towards the whole situation itself. What is called for in faith is an interiorly graced reorganization of the human spirit: "Be converted!" Jesus tells us, "and believe the good news—the kingdom of God is at hand!"

What will that mean in view of the economic arrangements in which we must live our lives? I will try to express what I think might be an overall answer here, leaving more detailed suggestions for a final chapter.

My proposal would be that, while (1) w e should always obtain the best counselling and healing available to us, the main choice we ought to make is (2) to share our littleness (our vulnerability) with others in a faith community whose members (3) trust primarily in the divine relationship in Christ, and only secondarily in technical achievements. But this spiritual attitude will not become meaningful and cannot become effective unless we are at the same time (4) taking part in the collective effort to bring about important changes in the economic system itself (aiming at the goal of justice).

There are four parts to this suggestion, but the third is the crucial one: Christian poverty for us (as in every age) must consist in giving primacy to the spiritual over the material order. In our modern situation this will mean gaining liberation from consumerism (as well as from all its addictive traps). Believers in Christ must seek ways of treating technologies and their products as means subordinated to spiritual ends. Our commitment to goals of the human spirit must break free from the chains of consumerism and addiction. That liberation should lead to a release of spiritual energies that are devoted to the pursuit of justice and compassionate love, both at home and abroad. Here, I believe, we are dealing with the essence of the matter.

The first point in my overall suggestion concerns healing in modern societies. This has become a major "industry" (a typical warp in our culture). Healing of many kinds is certainly necessary, but it can also become a dangerous form of self-centredness, and an extension of t he self-preoccupation that brings about psychic wounding in the first place.

As a result, I propose that we should always name our healing programs explicitly as secondary, and not allow them to become the main event in anyone's life. Healing, in short, is for well ness, and wellness enables us to devote our lives to meaningful and valuable goals. Despite what many keep repeating, I believe that we do not always need more healing. Long before our basic healing needs have been met, we should eagerly strain forward to take part in life as fully as we can—even if not entirely healed (for perhaps we will never be entirely healed in this life).

The second point in my suggested response brings forward the communal dimension that is always involved in Christian poverty. Even when not adverted to, the community exerts its influence out of sight. Human beings are not fully human except as members of society. There are no poor members of a rich society: a few may live more simply than others, but all share in the social system to which they belong.

Moreover, no matter how strong some members may appear to be, all of us are weak and vulnerable in our very nature. We may prefer not to admit it, but deep down we are aware of this fact—it's a part of being human. So we need to find forms of belonging which will nourish us in our littleness and overcome the serious dangers of isolation that threaten us in our modern situation.

That's why our sense of Christian poverty should include the communal dimension explicitly, I think. It's true for much else in our lives as well, but in the economic domain that we are considering here it's quite essential. As individuals, even if very self-assured (that is, even if we have developed a strong sense of self-worth in the best meaning of the term), there is very little we can do apart from others.

Most of our difficulties, in fact, are collective in character and call for collective responses. Our new awareness of what poverty means can be gained securely only by bouncing our ideas off others, receiving their support and their considered responses, and by helping one another to form new attitudes (with the assistance of divine grace). Without a concerned group to work and worship with, any efforts we try to make will likely be undermined by failures and discouragement.

The third point (the crucial one) has to do with making production subordinate to spiritual goals. A key feature of my overall response, it should be evident, concerns our ability to devote our energies effectively to technological efforts in the modern economy. This must include the collective effort to change its structures in new, spiritual directions. We can avoid the current tendency to become swallowed up in the machinery, to become part of a false system.

Should commercial ads tell us who we are and what our lives mean? If not, then what authentic goals do we choose to seek on earth? How can the wonderful gifts of modern technology be redirected to those ends? After all, we know that the material arrangements of life are intended to be means, directed to ends, freely determined by the human spirit. But, sad to say, the opposite is usually the case with us: the means have become an end in themselves, or the means decide what the end shall be.

To move this point into a more positive form, we could say that we choose to receive from God, our Creator and Saviour, the meaning and value of our lives. Even here on earth (that is, without considering our eternal destiny in heaven), we are called to build together a way of life that recognizes the worth of every person, the key importance of our environment and the conditions that will enable relationships of respect, compassion and justice to prevail.

Those spiritual goals are true in a general way for all the nations on earth as well as for ourselves where we live. But by embracing them and giving them primacy in our sense of who we are, we will soon discover more proximate goals for our own undertakings. In very practical ways we will be pulled beyond our own needs into the struggle for what can be done (within the reach of our hands) in the years ahead of us—working together to move us all in the direction of our common goals.

This more positive expression of my overall suggestion brings us to the fourth point, where we grasp how the economic system actually affects all members of society, especially the weakest, the disadvantaged and marginalized ones, and we grasp the need to change its structures. The positive statement of my suggestion implies the key importance of social justice as the aim of our time. As mentioned above, our secular awareness that our own social institutions—including economic ones—have been put into place historically by human beings will enable us to take up the task of changing their structures and their ways of operating in the direction of justice and compassion.

In my next and final chapter I will take up more detailed suggestions, practical attitudes which are focused on responding more effectively to "hard times."

5

How Can We Respond Today?

———————

Summing things up, we have been looking at current opinions about the hard times we are experiencing, at the teachings of Jesus on poverty in the Gospels, and at medieval efforts to put his teachings into practice. Then (in our last chapter) we have tried to bring out what is special about our own economic situation. Perhaps we could say briefly that the challenge we are facing involves an onslaught of consumerism and the psychic damage symbolized for us by enslaving addictions.

But in what practical ways should we try to give a truly spiritual response to this challenge of our time? Where exactly does our Christian faith lead us, together with others, in coming to grips with our highly organized world?

At the end of my previous chapter I attempted to express the response I have in mind—but only in general terms. I argued that we must seek to free ourselves from the golden chains of consumerism and to be healed of the psychic damages we have suffered. But while taking advantage of the best healing and counselling available to us, our spiritual choice must be to subordinate all our human technologies as means to the greater goal of divine service. This worship of God will always take the form of seeking justice in compassionate love for others in this world.

Now it is time to put some flesh on these bones. What could they amount to in actual practice?

In what follows I will make seven suggestions (none of them entirely new, of course) which I hope will be useful for all sorts of readers—whatever may be the circumstances in which they find themselves at present. Each suggestion for action will address a specific obstacle (the one it is meant to overcome) and will be accompanied by a practicum, an activity designed to assist each person to form the desired habit. I will also try to clarify the special virtue aimed at in practising the suggestion given.

1. Adopting A Simple Lifestyle

Since this is so often mentioned almost at once, it seems best to deal with it first. While it is helpful, it cannot pretend to be anything like an overall solution to what is called for. All the same, I think it deserves serious attention.

Like many of my other suggestions, it will vary for each person. A "simple lifestyle" is always going to be relative to the particular circumstances in which we actually live. Here I am thinking mainly of people in the more developed nations. (For most of us living here, to adopt the lifestyle of persons in less developed economies would be quite a shock.)

But compared to the much richer way I might live if I tried hard for it, a simple lifestyle would be several notches down the pole for me. That's the easiest way to indicate what is meant. It's up to each individual to decide concretely what this might entail.

It means noticeably less than what our commercial ads tell us we should seek. Since consumerism is our main obstacle in trying to develop a realistic approach to Christian poverty today, it is over against consumerist attitudes that a simple lifestyle may be grasped and realized.

False voices, false pressures in our society urge us to earn more money so as to buy more commodities, to commit ourselves to long-term payment obligations in order to get hold of what we can't afford right now, and so on. "See if you can't move up to a higher level of income/ownership." Or (since things are getting worse financially these days), "Perhaps another paying job could enable you to maintain your expensive mode of living? Why not try some moon-lighting?"

Unemployed people and all those living "below the poverty line" (a phrase used in the more developed world for persons at the lower levels of income in our society) will already have adopted "a simple lifestyle" whether they want it or not. For them, the question is whether they will choose to make spiritual goals their primary aim (even while continuing to seek a better income) or whether resentment, bitterness, discouragement, blaming, or depressed feelings will tend to dominate them.

When those negative states prevail (on the surface or just below the surface of their minds), a desire for material commodities still has primacy in their heart. Now, I don't think we ever have the right to criticize persons struggling with difficulties of that kind, much less to judge them morally. In any case, their condition may be temporary. And a new spiritual attitude, which might help to liberate them, usually comes about by means of God's grace—not through anyone else's efforts.

Materialistic pressures are mounting in our society as a whole, and the tensions we feel are getting so excessive that our health is sometimes in danger of being undermined. And so the suggestion that we deliberately adopt a simple lifestyle is meant to deal directly with this obstacle. It involves a choice. It should mean a carefully considered turn-around in our real attitude towards getting and spending. To repeat, only the grace of God will assist us truly to desire it and then to choose it effectively.

As a practicum aimed at solidifying this new attitude, a regular experience of contact with disadvantaged persons or groups is recommended. The purpose is to identify oneself with those living at the margin, rather than with those trying to move upward financially. It means learning to place one's real heart with the economically poor instead of with the rich.

This practicum calls for ongoing experiences, not a rare or occasional visit. It insists on solidarity of hearts and minds; it is not a matter of slumming as a "lord or lady bountiful," who condescends to be friendly with those beneath them. We should come to marginalized members of our society as equals, but as equals who have a lot to learn.

We are trying to form a new habit, a whole new sense of what life means. We are trying to get free from the bonds—and the accompanying lies—of the consumerist mentality. Except for a miracle of grace, it will not come quickly. (Even after the big grace of conversion, there will be much patient learning to be done in the months and years that follow.)

The virtue intended here is a greater trust in God alone for a deep sense of economic security. That is what Jesus is driving at when he asks, Why are you anxious? The flowers don't worry, and yet the Father clothes them. The birds don't worry, and yet God sees that they are fed. Your life is worth much more to God than birds or flowers (see Luke 12:22-24). Our Lord is concerned to free us from economic anxiety—not to tell us that we needn't make serious efforts to solve our economic problems.

2. Adopting The Goal Of Social Justice

Our obstacle in this case is self-absorption. People in the less developed parts of the world, who often live with an economic system operating at a quasi-agricultural level, are much less self-absorbed than those in the more developed world tend to be. Some in our own culture aggressively exploit us for economic reasons by appealing to our intensified sense of self.

In less developed nations the poorest people care for one another more than our members do, for the most part. It's quite noticeable. Without asking questions, they share the little they have. (Their richer members often appear quite indifferent.)

But to a great extent we seem to have lost our spontaneous feeling for others, and now we need to cultivate it. Perhaps when a serious situation of crisis is brought home to us emotionally we can be generous enough. But when that emergency has passed, we tend to lapse back into our habitual self-centredness. We become turned in on ourselves again. Our "next pleasure" seems terribly important to us. From extremes of Victorian puritanism in the nineteenth century we have gone all the way to the opposite extreme of "the ME-society."

That false spiritual attitude should be countered by choosing a new one: to change the unjust structures of our world, and to begin at once by desiring to change the false processes and institutions of our own society. This is meant in the sense of what is long-term and systemic: not merely to sing a nice song at a time of crisis ("We are the World, We are the Children"), but to change a system itself which is basically unjust.

To face a change of this size is not easy. In practice I've found that when individuals begin to take up this task they tend to be overwhelmed by the immensity of the problems. As soon as they openly seek to learn about human injustice (let alone our own involvement in it), they undergo the heavy desolation of too much bad news. It's more than human beings can take at first. There are limits to what we can bear.

True enough. But we can surmount those first difficulties when we get free of too much isolated responsibility, laying a heavy sense of guilt on our own backs. Instead, we could soon move forward to a sense of collective sinfulness, a growing awareness of original sin as it takes shape in our world. After a time this can lead us to a new hopefulness: I am coming to know what God has known all along. It is the divine Lord who bears the main brunt of this burden—I merely consent to share it.

And so we may receive the grace of committing our lives to the pursuit of social justice in ways that may lie within reach of our hands. In order to support a commitment of this kind, an essential practicum (it seems to me) would be to find a daily time of personal prayer. Especially effective would be a habit of interior prayer—any method that enables us to get into immediate contact with the divine mystery. With many people, daily prayer with others in a group will do as well.

When we set aside half an hour each day for what matters most to us—our relationship with the merciful God who cares passionately for all creatures—then we may grow to peace of heart in contemplating the enormous tasks facing us in our time. The virtue I have in mind here is one not usually given a name, a habit of openness and freedom in responding to the evils of the world in which we are called to live out our lives.

It's my conviction that the special framework of daily one-to-one contact with God in Christ is basic to every believer's commitment to social justice. That alone will liberate them from burnout, from false arrogance towards others, and from taking too much upon themselves. A combination of openness and freedom of this kind is needed if we are to persevere in the service of a faith that truly desires and seeks justice.

3. Joining A Support Community

In this instance I am thinking especially of the dangers of isolation, of personal weakness which we feel must be hidden from others—or even denied and concealed from oneself. It isn't enough to have one or two intimate friends (who know everything about me). No, I believe it's essential to belong to a group of others who share the same values and who meet together regularly to listen patiently and to support one another.

Modern culture has tended, on one hand, to hold up an ideal of individual strength and heroism (the frontier marshall) and, on the other, to break down the bonds of true community. This exposes anyone who follows such an ideal to self-deceptions of the worst kind. Where they lead eventually is to despair—at least to discouragement, despondency or cynicism. For we are not naturally meant to be heroes and heroines. Rather, we are meant to become truthful among close friends who continue to affirm our worth even when our weaknesses and limitations are revealed to them (compassionate love).

The practicum in this case would be learning to share one's real, interior and day-to-day events with a small group of companions. For some people, this will require repeated efforts and some failures before its true benefits begin to appear.

The new ability involved is the virtue of belonging. It sees that to become more fully humanized is to know one's need for membership with other persons. Community at the local level is essential to the human condition. Our faith in Christ's presence among us will enable us to belong deeply and enduringly.

4. Self-worth As Prior To Any Performance

Another major obstacle facing us in hard times comes from the false doctrines of the "Puritan Ethic," especially the notion that we have to prove ourselves by accomplishing something. It imagines that high standards of performance are set over our heads, and that our value as persons will be judged by whether or not we measure up or can "reach the top."

Since only one or a very few will ever reach the top, all the rest of us can seem to be second-rate. It's worse when we make this kind of judgment against ourselves. Then we nearly always feel worthless. We are failures in our own eyes, or we are in constant danger of failing to achieve any real value in the eyes of others.

A practicum which may help to develop our sense of self-worth as prior to any actions might consist in celebrating the gifts of creation by God and salvation in Christ. Those are the greatest gifts we have and they are given us without any merit on our part. We can thank God for them in many ways—at morning prayer as we wake up to a new day, at grace before meals, on feasts and anniversaries, at special moments with others. When it's more urgently needed (in the case of this or that person), it could be practised often each day—for example, when moving from one event to the next.

Whatever forms the practicum of celebrating life may take, the virtue aimed at here is gratitude, which is the basic stance of believers in the presence of God.

This virtue, when it has become a lively one, does not mean that we have no ideals or that we perform no effective actions. No, it means the contrary: our true ideals are not "over our heads, threatening us now," but set in front of us as goals for realistic and persevering action. For we are pilgrims (as we saw) on a journey that has a glorious destination.

We are going somewhere that matters to us. That means not merely being but also doing. "Good fruit comes from a good tree," says Jesus (Mt 7:17). What we do is not needed to prove that we have any worth. Instead, our sense of worth as created and saved by the God who passionately cares for us enables us to perform excellent actions—and we eagerly do so. Because we are relaxed about our personal worth, we can joyfully pour out our energies in doing what is worthwhile.

5. Self-worth As Independent Of Income

Another difficulty in attaining self-worth comes, I believe, mainly from the materialistic warp in modern culture of treating persons as though they were things. In our economic system this warped attitude leads to measuring the value of each person by the level of his or her income. It's so deep-rooted and so persistent that we tend to do it to ourselves.

As soon as anyone loses a job, for instance, or even has to take a cut in salary, the person often falls into self-doubt. "Is it because I'm no good? Is something wrong with me as a human being? Will I be a failure in everyone's eyes from now on?" These awful doubts are not reasonable, but they dominate our deep feelings, if not our minds.

It's important to get free of this warped attitude, then, and as a means to it I suggest the practicum of an imagined "downward mobility." By this I mean a deliberate choice that runs directly counter to the materialistic view of human worth so current in our world. Choose to imagine yourself in various positions of low income.

If it bothers you to do so, keep at it until you feel calmer and can come to accept it. Share your struggle (if you are, in fact, struggling) with friends and companions. In other words, try to identify your true self with your spiritual values and not with your level of income. (I assume it is clear I don't mean that we shouldn't earn our living or cease to make sensible arrangements for our material needs and for those who depend on us. Obviously, those duties always remain. But I think we should strive to get free of any notion that our material needs come first, or define who we are, or can rightly be used to measure our worth as human beings.)

The aim of testing ourselves with "downward mobility" is to acquire the virtue of spiritual poverty itself, as I understand Jesus to teach it in the Gospel. We should imagine ourselves as intensely as we can to be severely handicapped, or suffering the consequences of a stroke, or to have lost our long-term job and unable to find a new one, and so on.

A religious sister who was severely handicapped by polio once told me about a woman friend who used to lean close to her at public meetings and whisper, "I'm handicapped, too." Both of them knew that the friend's handicap was psychic, not physical. This became a joke between them, much appreciated. The fact was that the sister had struggled for years to get free of any limitations on her service of others, and had received this grace abundantly.

Keep on doing this exercise, then, in order to reach the spiritual condition of one who rejoices in freedom from any anxiety over questions of self-worth and feels committed to goals higher than material concerns. These goals will include, of course, the intention of working with others collectively to make the economic system itself subordinate to the spiritual values of justice and compassion.

6. Stewardship In The Use Of Possessions

In the teeth of Western culture's excessive stress on individual ownership rights, the Church has frequently raised the issue of common rights. In other words, property and goods belong, not only to the individuals who own them, but also to the society that dwells in the land as a whole. It's not that the Church has not championed the right and the need of individuals and families to own private property—that has always been a solid part of her teaching. It's just that the excessive individualism of modern views has needed to be balanced by reminders of community rights.

For example, we are told that in the eighteenth century thieves were condemned to death for stealing a rabbit, or other small items like that. Robbery is wrong, but is ownership of the rabbit more important than the life of the thief? Something was badly out of balance in that notion of "justice."

Similarly, the doctrine of laissez-faire in the nineteenth century led governments to irresponsible acts of non-interference when merchants shipped food out of the country at the same time that many individuals were starving to death. This may seem to be an extreme case, hard to understand today, but at least it illustrates how one-sided the emphasis on individual ownership can become. That false emphasis itself continues to influence many minds today.

The term "stewardship" may serve us well in this context. What I own is for myself and my family, of course, but since it is also partly meant for the whole community, I can come to see myself as a steward of its rightful use. The same may be extended to the whole world today: we are the first generation growing into global awareness of all other peoples as a single population living precariously on the resources of our common planet, Earth. Economic decisions made in one part influence the whole world.

And so, taken together, we are meant to be joint stewards of the material resources at our common disposal. The market for all kinds of goods is now worldwide. On the longer term, no segments of the world's population can continue to consume the lion's share and feast to superfluity while the majority remains close to physical destitution or mired in underdevelopment. Anyone who reflects carefully on these matters knows that we cannot continue very long in the way we have been going.

It follows that at home in the West we need to seek freedom from our habits of "selfish ownership." More positively, we must learn how to become true stewards of God's good creation. What practicum might enable us to develop the new attitude required? In our local societies we might make it a norm to "include a stranger at every feast." An example might be to invite persons who seem to be left out of ordinary communities (for whatever reason), asking them as a favour to become part of our celebrations.

A few years ago I was a privileged guest at my nephew's Christmas party. I found myself chatting with an older man who lived in the forest nearby. He had no family of his own, and few contacts in the neighbourhood. Obviously, too, his income was very limited. It was an enjoyable discussion since he clearly felt right at home and happy to celebrate Christmas with a joyful family group. Later I was shown the abandoned trailer where he lived in the woods. My nephew and his wife had discovered his isolation and wanted to include him in their party. They would have felt uneasy if he had spent his Christmas alone.

This example of God's grace at work in a family is meant to illustrate the sense of stewardship I think we all need to cherish in our hearts. It's not a sense of "kindness" or "charity," so much as a feeling for what is right. Many readers have already developed this attitude, I'm certain, and so I wish merely to put it into the spotlight for a moment so as to recognize its value and recommend it for the global society to which we belong.

7. Contributing One's Special Gift

As a final suggestion for developing an effective spirituality for hard times, I would like to put forward the conviction that every person without exception has "a special gift" to bring to human society. It derives from the divine creation and the event of salvation in Christ, already mentioned above. Each person, then, should be encouraged to find what that special giftedness might be and to contribute it to others.

As experience can teach us, some of the best gifts received in any society come from quieter members—gifts of listening, of taking time to reflect together, doing ordinary daily tasks, finding out what shy persons need, caring for the sick or the elderly or ailing members, and so on. More spectacular gifts need less attention since they are already well recognized. But the community which "includes" every member will make sure that all of them believe in their own contributions and gain recognition in the whole community.

Many readers familiar with St. Paul's epistles (see I Cor. 12:20-26) will recall how much he insists on this idea: "There are many members, yet one body. The eye cannot say to the hand, 'I have no need of you,' nor again the hand to the feet, 'I have no need of you.' On the contrary, the members of the body that seem to be weaker are indispensable" (vv.20-22).

Now, not everyone feels this way about herself or himself. Many simply expect others to tell them what they ought to do with their lives. And many others don't know what their own special gift might be. They haven't discovered it yet. Or they've become discouraged because of the hurts received in life, the set-backs to their growth and the failures they've had to deal with. Perhaps others see themselves as wounded members of society, as helpless victims or as so severely handicapped that there is nothing they can give.

Contrary to all those defeatist attitudes, I protest that we must first of all believe in our worth and then find what we can give. The giving will be much easier when we first believe. In fact, the giving of our own gift will almost look after itself. It may come spontaneously when we've begun to believe deeply enough in our own special qualities as human beings.

Jesus Christ tells us (in effect): "Don't believe the bad news. Believe the good news!" There's no lack of bad news in our world today. We are so aware of all the things that can go wrong that we can become locked into the negatives, entrenched in defensive positions, keeping our guard up against anything else that may come our way. That's "believing the bad news."

This is a form of non-faith, perhaps, but very effective in preventing anything better from coming about. It shows the power of faith—even in what is false, giving it control as long as we continue to believe in it.

With a negative attitude of that sort the hard times we are going through can appear to be nothing but "bad news," nothing but a ticket to unhappiness and misery. But Our Lord tries to teach us (to call forth from our hearts by his grace) a very different spiritual attitude: "Believe the good news!" Trust in God's help. Leave the defensive "trench warfare" mentality of the First World War, and free your life-energies for the important task of making a constructive contribution. In other words, find your own special gift and set your heart on contributing it to others.

A serious obstacle here is the widespread notion in our media that, after we've done what we have to do in our working time, we should expect to be entertained in our leisure moments. This implies that work is a boring drudgery and free time is meant for "the fun society."

This is a big topic in itself, and I will not launch into it here (I'm not opposed to good humour and enjoyment!), but I do want to express my belief that the attitude just mentioned gets everything upside down. However common it may be, it presents a topsy-turvy view of reality. The whole of our life should be joyful. We should not expect to have "fun" only in leisure times. Peace should pervade everything we do, work as well as recreation. Peace and joy are meant to be normal for those who believe in Christ; pain and trouble are facts, but exceptional.

The "entertainment" view of life (the idea that we need to be "distracted" and "amused" all the time) comes from the fact that for so many people what they do is empty and meaningless for them. This is not the fault of most individuals—it's what they have to face in their actual situation. But my point here is that we are called in faith to turn this around. At least, we can begin to do so and to encourage one another in this aim.

A practicum that might assist this effort is a pretty obvious one—volunteering. Many active people are doing a lot of this already, and it's not a cure-all. Perseverance will be needed by each person to find the right tasks. A number of early tries may turn out negatively. Sometimes it's only by actually doing something that we discover what it's like and whether it's right for us in particular.

If you're so busy already that you have no time for volunteering, then I suggest that you choose to do whatever you are doing in a spirit of freedom and joyfulness—rather than taking it as an imposition, a heavy burden laid on your back.

What I am stressing are the attitudes we can bring to our main work and to our volunteer jobs. That is where spirituality comes in. Our convictions about happiness, about our own worth and about the special gift we have to contribute to others—all these need to be "discouragement proof." Arrows of bad news that come our way should fall to the ground without leaving a dent on our joyful purpose.

The virtue to be sought in this connection might be named "self-forgetfulness." It's a well-known truth that we discover happiness not when we seek it directly for ourselves, but when we plunge into action for others. When we forget ourselves in doing what seems worthwhile we may gradually realize—in the middle of doing it, or afterwards in reflection—how much more we have received, how truly happy we've become through that very forgetfulness of our own self and our own troubles.

In conclusion, may I say that I hear much of this in the mysterious saying of Jesus: "Whoever wants to save his own life will lose it; but whoever loses his life for me and for the gospel will save it" (Mark 8:35).

As he looked about his world at that time, Christ Our Lord saw many suffering people, many struggling hopelessly with their economic difficulties—in short, enduring hard times. His teaching about poverty of spirit was meant not to provide a practical solution in economic terms, but instead to enable them to work confidently and joyfully in taking up the tasks of life together.

Let us all pray for one another to receive the grace of doing this in the hard times we are facing today.

Recommended Reading

(Annotated)

Poverty in the New Testament

Hengel, Martin. *Earliest Christianity.* Tr. J. Bowden. London: SCM Press, 1986 (German orig., 1973). In a key chapter (pp. 171-178), Hengel contrasts Jesus' radical criticism of property-owners with his open acceptance of ownership. Two further chapters (pp. 179-182, 183-189) deal with the primitive Christians in Acts and in Paul's Epistles. The author is very clear on the special economic situations of the New Testament period.

Lohfink, Gerhard. *Jesus and Community.* Tr. J. Galvin. New York: Paulist, 1984 (German orig., 1982). This is an excellent discussion of the newer understanding of the Lord's situation in Palestine. The key difference between "travelling" and "settled" disciples is emphasized.

Nolan, Albert. *Jesus Before Christianity.* Maryknoll, N.Y.: Orbis, 1976. The social make-up of the Lord's hearers, and especially the bearing of his teaching on the contemporary situation in Palestine, is clearly developed in this compelling study.

Historical Forms of Christian Poverty

Hengel, Martin. *Earliest Christianity* (as above), especially Part 2, "Property and Riches in the Early Church," pp. 147-244, brings forward material not easily available elsewhere. The author makes evident (1) how difficult the Lord's teaching was to embody in actual social conditions then, and (2) how very different that cultural epoch was from later, and especially our modern, societies.

Knowles, David. "Religious Poverty: Traditional Approaches." *The Way, Supplement 9* (1970), 16-26. This article contrasts Benedictine and Franciscan forms of vowed poverty.

Little, Lester K. *Religious Poverty and the Profit Economy in Medieval Europe.* Ithaca, N.Y.: Cornell, 1978. I consider this fine study to be required reading for anyone who wishes to understand the emergence of Western civilization and especially the meaning of Franciscan and Dominican forms of Christian poverty.

O'Malley, John W., SJ. "The Jesuits, St. Ignatius, and the Counter Reformation." *Studies in the Spirituality of Jesuits* 14 (no.1). St. Louis: Seminar in Jes. Spir., 1982. Excellent historical material for grasping special Ignatian contributions made at the time.

Osuna, Francisco de, OFM. *The Third Spiritual Alphabet.* Tr. M. Giles. New York: Paulist, 1981. An early sixteenth-century classic on "recollection" for lay persons who wished to develop their Christian lives in the world.

Outram, H. Evennett. *The Spirit of the Counter-Reformation.* Cambridge: Cambridge University Press, 1968. Background understanding for the rise of Jesuit influence in the later sixteenth century.

The Contemporary Situation

Brzezinski, Zbigniew. *Out of Control: Global Turmoil on the Eve of the 21st Century.* New York: Maxwell Macmillan, 1993. The author finds the root danger in the spiritual void of the consumer culture of the West, and calls for spiritual renewal.

Canadian Conference of Catholic Bishops. *Ethical Choices and Political Challenges.* Ottawa: CCCB, 1983. A very practical and readable plea for public action in favour of the economically poor in our time.

Canadian Conference of Catholic Bishops. *Widespread Unemployment: A Call to Mobilize the Social Forces of Our Nation.* Ottawa: Episcopal Commission for Social Affairs, CCCB, 1993. This *cri de coeur* gives urgency to a spiritual transformation of our leaders, and of all citizens, in addressing the current crisis in un- and under-employment.

Holland, Joe, and Peter Henriot, SJ. *Social Analysis: Linking Faith and Justice.* Rev. ed. Maryknoll, N.Y.: Orbis, 1983. Shows how our new sense of social justice becomes central to the practice of Christian poverty.

Kavanaugh, John F., SJ. *Following Christ in a Consumer Society.* Maryknoll, N.Y.: Orbis, 1982. Imaginatively presented insights into contemporary difficulties for Christian poverty.

Kerans, Patrick. *Sinful Social Structures.* New York, Toronto: Paulist, 1974. A brief study of the new "structural awareness" of our time.

Mantoux, Paul. *The Industrial Revolution in the Eighteenth Century.* Evanston, N.Y.: Harper & Row, 1961 (French orig., 1928). This classic story gives the origins of the immense technological changes soon to sweep over Europe and North America, and later to dominate the entire globe.

National [U.S.A.] Council of Catholic Bishops. *Economic Justice for All: Catholic Social Teaching and the U.S. Economy.* Washington, D.C.: U.S. Catholic Conference, 1986 (see *Origins,* 16 (1986), 408-456). A serious effort to apply Christian moral principles to recent difficulties in poverty and unemployment.

Rahner, Karl, SJ. "Poverty." In *Contemporary Spirituality,* ed. by R. Gleason, 45-78. New York: Macmillan, 1969. Originally written in 1960 (prior to Vatican Council II), these perceptive essays, although mostly restricted to poverty as practised in vowed communities, discuss the difficulties in trying to locate our traditional principles in the economic conditions of modern Western culture.

Practical Needs Today

Baltaz, Diane P. *Living Off the Land: A Spirituality of Farming.* Ottawa: Novalis, 1991. This readable essay brings forward data on the lives of small farmers today, and presents the attempts of several groups to develop rural lifestyles in modern conditions.

"Poverty, and a Poverty of Analysis." *Toronto Globe and Mail,* Dec. 29, 1992, Sect. A, p. 18. This piece explains the notion of the "poverty line" and what is wrong with it: "defining poverty as income insufficient to purchase healthy food, decent clothing and adequate shelter would surely be far superior . . . ."

Tucker, Graham. *The Faith-Work Connection.* Toronto: Anglican Book Centre, 1987. A down-to-earth, realistic treatment (useful for group discussions) of faith-approaches to marketplace needs and programs. The author explicitly includes businessmen within his target readership.